ChiWalking

Also by Danny Dreyer and Katherine Dreyer

ChiRunning

ChiWalking

THE FIVE MINDFUL STEPS FOR
LIFELONG HEALTH AND ENERGY

Danny Dreyer

and Katherine Dreyer

POCKET
BOOKS

LONDON • SYDNEY • NEW YORK • TORONTO

First published in Great Britain by Pocket Books, 2009
An imprint of Simon & Schuster UK Ltd
A CBS COMPANY

Copyright © Danny Dreyer, 2006

ChiRunning and ChiWalking are registered trademarks
of ChiLiving, Inc.

www.simonsays.co.uk

Simon & Schuster Australia
Sydney

A CIP catalogue record for this book is
available from the British Library

ISBN: 978-1-84739-279-4

Designed by Chris Welch
Printed by CPI Cox & Wyman, Reading, Berkshire RG1 8EX

To our daughter,
The Journey is the reward.
—Chinese proverb

Acknowledgments

We would like to thank the many people who have supported the creation of this book.

First and foremost we want to thank our neighbors and dear friends Sarah, David, and Sidney Leipsic, who support us in so many ways and mostly by being a second family to our daughter, Journey. Your friendship and support of our family are invaluable.

Anne, our hardworking gentle-spirited angel of an office manager, who supports us in so many ways . . . you have our deep gratitude.

Master Xu, we are forever indebted to you for your patience and your generosity with teaching us about Chi and how to bring it into our lives and the lives of others. This book would not have happened without you.

Many thanks to Kathy Griest and Chris Griffin, Master ChiRunning and ChiWalking instructors. Working with you both is an honor.

And many thanks to all the ChiRunning and ChiWalking Certified Instructors for your incredible dedication to healthy movement and for helping others move from their centers.

Bonnie Solow, our agent who had faith in us from the start, thanks for believing. There is a long list of those at Simon & Schuster we want to thank: Chris Lloreda, we are so grateful for your support and belief in us; Doris Cooper, your words of encouragement gave us the energy to bring this book to completion and your editing was right on target; Lisa Sciambra, we owe you so much for helping get the word about the Chi books out to the public; Nancy Inglis, for fine-tuning the book; and many thanks to all those in the design and production departments who make the book beautiful.

We also want to thank Marge Thomas, our family health practitioner, who cares for us physically, mentally, emotionally, and spiritually. Marge, you are a bright light in our lives and keep us focused and healthy to do the work we need to do. Tim and Jane Heintzelman, thanks for guiding us always toward the truth.

Dear Dr. Betty Smith, our first official ChiRunning Ambassador. You are an amazing light in our lives. Ozzie Gontang, your support has meant a lot to us. It has been so helpful to have your many years of experience confirm that ChiWalking is headed in the right direction. Jim Dunn: Danny's best friend, and Journey's first crush—need we say more? We love you.

Many thanks to the readers of our first book, *ChiRunning*, for your feedback and encouragement, and for spreading the word. It is all of you who gave us the inspiration to write this book.

And thanks to our parents and siblings, incredibly inspiring and endlessly supportive. We're deeply grateful for all you have done and continue to do. And last, but most important, to Journey. Wow! We are so lucky to be your parents and to watch you grow. Words cannot express our love.

Contents

Chapter 7. Creating Your ChiWalking Program   177

Chapter 8. Hiking: Welcome to Off-road Walking   194

Chapter 9. Indoor Walking and the Mindful Treadmill   219

Chapter 10. Creating Balance in Your Diet   229

Chapter 11. The Choice Is Yours   245

Index   251

The Upward Spiral
of Chi

'll never forget being in Ireland thirty some years ago, stretching
my legs on a nice walk in the glorious, early-spring countryside.
After spending fourteen and a half hours cooped up in a trans-
atlantic flight the day before, I was primed for a vigorous outing. I was
living in Boulder at the time and was trying to wean myself off of unnecessary driving. As a result, I had taken up walking as a way to learn
to slow myself down and add some spaciousness to my life. I was "between jobs" so I took the opportunity to explore the country where, I
had been told, my ancestors on my mother's side of the family once
lived.

As I began my walk, I noticed an older gentleman about 200 yards
ahead of me, apparently also out for a walk. Young and out to prove
myself, I challenged myself to catch up with him and seize the oppor-

tunity to meet one of the "locals." I knew I'd have to walk a bit faster, but I was confident that within a short time I'd be on his heels.

Forget it.

Try as I might, I soon realized that he was pulling away from me, and even though he was at least twenty years my senior, he seemed to be disappearing into the distance. After about ten minutes of this nonsense, I gave up my quest, totally humbled.

So much for meeting a local and so much for thinking I was a fit walker.

In the following days, I noted that most people in Ireland walked as a matter of course. They were all fit beyond belief, and their faces sparkled with rosy cheeks and that zest for life for which the Irish are famous. Walking, I came to realize, was in their blood and played a large part in keeping them healthy and happy—along with their music, storytelling, and ale, of course. That trip to Ireland was when I first allowed walking to have a sacred status in my life. I saw it for the vital, long-term value that it offers.

When I was in New York City recently, I felt a nice sense of camaraderie with the people on the street. They were all walking. I'm sure the reason was not so much for its health reasons, but because walking is often the most convenient way to get from one part of Manhattan to another. I observed what seemed like an unusually high percentage of physically fit people. But contrary to the Bay Area, where I teach walking classes, New Yorkers don't dwell on how much walking they do, they just accept walking as a part of life. They do it because they have to, and most of them inadvertently end up in better shape because of it. It's the nature of walking.

Marjorie, my 86-year-old neighbor, goes out for her ritual walk, rain or shine, twice every day for 30 to 45 minutes. She's in amazing shape for her age. She still lives alone in her home of fifty years and drives her friends to their doctor's appointments. She volunteers time at the public library, takes herself to church every Sunday, and cat-sits for us when we're out of town. She tells me that walking is her connection to living a healthy and vibrant life, and says that she's thankful for every day that she wakes up and goes out for her walk. Marjorie sees the incredible benefit that walking provides. It's as important to her as going to church—and it should be. It inspires her mind, activates her body, and nourishes her soul.

In our first book, *ChiRunning: A Revolutionary Approach to Effortless, Injury-free Running,* we wanted to share with runners the potential for running without the pain and injury that everyone associates with running.

In this book we are coming back to our first love, walking. And in chapter 8 of this book, we share perhaps our favorite activity, hiking. In writing this book, Katherine and I both realized what a powerful impact walking has had on our lives. Katherine has been a walker most of her life, spending countless hours as a teenager walking and exploring Connecticut with her dog. I have spent some of the most joyous times in my life hiking and discovering myself and the beauty of the Colorado Rockies, where I spent most of my life. When Katherine moved to Colorado, she too spent every weekend exploring the high country.

(Although Katherine and I have written this book together, whenever you see "I," it's me, Danny speaking. When Katherine's speaking, we'll indicate it, and when you see "we" it's from both of us.)

Walking is a wonderful thing and a natural part of many people's lives. In many European countries it is common to take an after-dinner walk. But whether you walk out of necessity, because you enjoy it, or because you're working toward improved health, it is *the* most accessible form of exercise on the planet—period. It gets you into great shape quickly and can have a dramatic impact on your immediate and long-term health.

For those who are looking to get started on a fitness program, it not only allows you to get started easily, painlessly, and joyfully, it also offers enormous, long-range potential.

ChiWalking can be adapted to any walking program and offers limitless possibilities for gaining mastery over your health and overall well-being.

GET ALIGNED WITH YOUR LIFE FORCE

In this book you'll be introduced to the most revolutionary approach to walking since the invention of walking shoes. We will explain the connection between chi and walking and how you can use walking to access this very powerful source of energy that is always available to you.

ChiWalking draws on principles borrowed from T'ai Chi, an ancient martial art based on the energetic balance of the body. In T'ai Chi, creating balance is both the means *and* the goal. The same is true for ChiWalking. For instance, you can create energetic balance in your life (the goal) by creating balance in your body with an aligned spine, a balanced walking form, and a great program (the means).

I went to my first T'ai Chi class ten years ago, on the recommendation of a friend. T'ai Chi had always held a fascination for me because I had wanted to explore my Chinese heritage from my father's side. As I walked into class that evening and watched Master Xilin leading the class in a most powerful yet graceful way, a remarkable feeling of "being home" swept over me. I felt that joyful sense of familiarity that comes when I run into an old friend on the street. I immediately knew that this was where I wanted to be. Over the next two years, I learned an entirely new way of relating to my body and to movement in general—a way that involved moving consciously from my center instead of haphazardly moving with no particular method in mind. When Katherine and I began applying these principles to our own walking and teaching others what we were discovering, we began to see truly remarkable results in a relatively short period. Aches and pains were disappearing. Our clients were noting that they could walk farther and faster with much greater ease and enjoyment. Our distance-walking clients were requiring no or greatly reduced recovery times. Since then I have seen thousands of people learn how to access and direct the flow of their energy (chi) by using the ChiWalking technique and reap the many benefits of creating balance and alignment in their lives. Here's a particularly exciting story from a retired colonel of the American armed forces, now working in Colombia against the proliferation of drugs:

Katherine,

I just returned from a week with the Colombian police locating and destroying cocaine labs. These labs are hidden deep in the jungle ravines.

The typical operation begins with a helicopter landing on a mountain ridgeline, followed by a steep descent to the lab. The lab is destroyed, and then the fun part begins with the ascent back up to the helicopter landing zone. Some of these ascents can take longer than an hour. The men carry 40 pounds of gear.

I applied your same principles to my "life" this week. I did not muscle my way up the hills; rather I "chi'd" my way up. I concentrated on the principles and focuses, not on the daunting task at hand. Result: the easiest week I have had since I started the job. Every morning I bounced out of bed ready to go, as if I had done nothing the day prior—unlike the 65 other people I was with.

After the second day, I shared your discoveries with my partner, and as you might expect, he had the same results. I plan to pass these points on to the Colombian police.

You probably should write another book for Mount Everest expeditions. —*Regards, Kevin*

I continue to study T'ai Chi in San Francisco with Master George Xu and am constantly reminded of the power of chi and the remarkable difference it can make to learn to direct this invisible force. According to the Chinese, chi (pronounced *chee*) is the life force that animates all things. It flows through your body along a system of meridians. They're like electric circuits that carry your chi energy throughout your body, most importantly to your internal organs, your muscles, and your lymphatic system. The existence of chi in the body cannot be measured with scientific instruments, but what *has* been documented are countless cases of the effectiveness of Chinese acupuncture in healing everything from incontinence to cancer. For generations, the Chinese have learned to sense and direct this subtle energy through the practices of T'ai Chi and Chi Gung. But let's be clear: you don't need to know how to do T'ai Chi to sense and to direct your chi. Through the ChiWalking exercises in this book, you will learn how to set up the right conditions for chi to circulate freely throughout your body, and you'll learn how to tap into this limitless source of energy by practicing these Five Mindful Steps in your walking. You don't even need to understand what chi is to practice ChiWalking. Nonetheless, you will be able to feel more abundant energy—and that's what matters most.

ALIGN YOUR BODY

I begin every walking class just as any good T'ai Chi teacher would, by focusing on posture and alignment. T'ai Chi and ChiWalking both start by teaching you good posture, just like your mother always tried to do. That's because good posture is the absolute foundation for all that will come later. You'll first learn to maintain great structural alignment that allows your muscles to relax and your chi energy to flow more freely through your body. When your posture is in alignment, the core muscles of your body are set to work and your arms and legs can take a backseat. You'll learn to walk not from leg strength, but from core strength, which is healthier because it exercises your entire body and more efficient because you are not relying solely on your legs to move you forward. Then, as you practice strengthening your physical core, you'll begin to sense an "inner strength" growing inside you that you can tap into anytime in your daily life.

ALIGN YOUR MIND

ChiWalking exercises your mind by asking you to focus on technique while leading the body through a workout. The ability to align your mind with your body is an essential ingredient to any successful fitness program. In ChiWalking we call this mind-body skill Body Sensing: your mind is "listening" to your body, then directing your body to make positive changes in its movement. You'll then listen again, and perhaps make another adjustment such as swinging your arms a bit more or holding your head higher. In this way you'll establish a communication link between your mind and body that allows you to create the kind of energy your body, mind, and spirit need. For example, if you're like me and tend to carry tension in your shoulders, you'll learn to relax your shoulders while you're walking by employing one of the many relaxation focuses from this book. Once your tension is gone, energy will again flow through your shoulders unobstructed, leaving you clearheaded and energized. What a concept!

GETTING PHYSICALLY FIT

Make no mistake: With ChiWalking, your walking program will first and foremost be an ongoing fitness program that will give you all the benefits that cardio-aerobic conditioning has to offer. We will show you how to walk your way to the best shape of your life by offering you a "menu" of different types of fitness walks (chapter 5).

ChiWalking will introduce you to an energizing and viable way to get fit and healthy without the strain, stress, and potential injury of many other sports. This is a *total* fitness program from which you can attain as high a level of fitness as you would like. Through ChiWalking you can condition your body in these five important ways for a lifelong physical fitness program:

1. Aerobic conditioning
   - Keeps your muscles young and healthy
   - Improves your oxygen uptake so that your muscles work more efficiently
2. Cardiovascular health
   - Builds a strong heart
   - Protects against heart disease
   - Increases blood flow to all muscles and organs
3. Muscle tone
   - Keeps you looking and feeling great
   - Contributes to improved balance
4. Flexibility
   - Allows ease of movement
   - Increases agility

5. Bone density
   • Guards against the onset of osteoporosis
   • Strengthens bones and reduces the risk of fracture

If you would like to have a great entryway into a safe, effective fitness program, this book is for you.

If you're looking for a great way to recover from injury, illness, or surgery, this book is also for you.

If you want to prepare for a hiking trip or a distance-walking event such as a marathon, ChiWalking will get you there.

If you want to use walking to develop a great body-mind connection, learn how to manage your energy, and unlock your hidden potential, then this program will knock your socks off!

GET ALIGNED BY MAKING THE BEST CHOICES

Getting physically fit is a choice you must make. It's not going to happen by accident.

This book is about making positive choices moment to moment in how you move physically and ultimately in how you manage your energy. It starts simply, and most important, in your physical body and from there integrates into your mind and your Being.

As I mentioned earlier, in T'ai Chi you start by aligning your spine and physical body to create a clear conduit for chi. Correct body alignment allows energy to flow to where it's needed. The same thing happens in everyday life. When you get "aligned" with your personal goals, whether to lose weight, or keep young, or reach the peak of a mountain, the energy to realize those goals is able to flow. I've received innumerable letters from people who have made the choice to get fit. ChiWalking has allowed them to move in a whole new healthy direction in their lives! Here's one:

Hi, Danny,
My wife has recently lost 10 lbs (I'm not supposed to tell anyone), and a big part of that is walking your way. After my session with you last month, I showed her the basics, and she began walking by

lifting and leaning. Now she walks every day, loves it, and goes for an hour or so at a time. Her heart rate is lower and she's not pounding hard. Overall she seems healthier and happier.

Thanks, —*Glenn*

THE UPWARD SPIRAL OF CHI

With chi flowing in your life, your energy expands and grows rather than spiraling downward like water whirlpooling down a drain. As you integrate the inner focuses of ChiWalking into your life, your chi, or life force, can flow unhampered through your body, and your life will move in an upward spiral like a hawk riding an updraft with ease and grace.

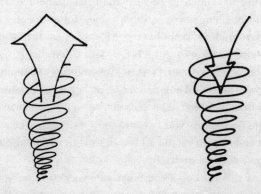

Figure 2a—Upward spiral   **Figure 2b—Downward spiral**

When energy flows in your body from relaxing and making positive choices, wonderful things happen: your joints, muscles, and ligaments move more freely; you have access to more energy; your mind becomes clear and focused; and your spirit gets renewed. When all this is going on, you are in a better position to make good choices. That's what we call the Upward Spiral of Chi, and it can get you on the right track with your health and overall well-being. The more good choices you make, the more energy you'll have. The more energy you have, the more inner strength you'll have to make better choices.

Here's another note I received from someone who has changed the direction of his health and life:

> I am a recovering smoker . . . I just want to thank you. I feel better and have brought chi into my life and things are looking up. Again, thank you for everything. —*Calvin*

HOW TO USE THIS BOOK

As you probably know, it's not always easy to stay on track with a fitness program. It sometimes seems as if the devil himself is plotting to keep you from exercising. Once you've read this book, you'll see that walking has much more to it than meets the eye. We've addressed this challenge by creating a wonderful menu of walks that engage your whole body and being. Most physical fitness programs are limited to just working the body. With ChiWalking, more than just your physical needs will be met. We're talking about physical fitness, mental fitness, and emotional fitness. You'll end each walk truly energized from head to toe because you've engaged your *whole* body and being. We'll show you twelve totally different walks that can challenge and inspire you on all levels, leaving you champing at the bit to get out the door each day.

Think of this book as a combination owner's manual and recipe book. Staying consistent and on track will be easy when you design your walking program with the principle of Gradual Progress in mind (chapter 4). It's all about being kind to yourself and not being in a hurry to change everything all at once. You'll develop a program that fits your needs, one that will keep you engaged and energized. The key to staying with any exercise program is to make it fun and interesting. The more you enjoy it, the more it becomes an integral part of your life (like the New Yorkers, the Irish, and Marjorie, about whom I spoke earlier).

I would suggest reading this book through once, just as a read. Then go back through it more carefully, taking notes and highlighting places that are particularly helpful. Then reread it at regular intervals to remind yourself of how far you've come. I'd also suggest using sticky tabs to locate all of your favorite focuses and walks described in the book. Just remember, the more accessible you can make your book, the more you'll use it. Consistent effort in building new habits will make positive change a certainty.

ChiWalking is a truly enjoyable way to get and stay healthy and fit, so let's get started.

CHAPTER ONE

Health Is the Goal, Movement Is the Key

Above all, do not lose your desire to walk. Every day I walk myself into a state of well-being and walk away from every illness. I have walked myself into my best thoughts, and I know of no thought so burdensome that one cannot walk away from it.—SØREN KIERKEGAARD

The crowds roared with enthusiasm as Edward Payson Weston crossed the finish line. People lined the streets to watch him and cheer him on. Weston was a leading sports figure of the nineteenth and twentieth centuries, an athlete who captured the hearts and attention of Americans and Europeans by walking long distances. During Weston's time, walking was a glamorous sport, and stadiums regularly filled with spectators for walking events and matches.

Weston was also a wonderful study for the doctors of the time. At age 67 he was examined by thirty doctors who found that his muscles, lungs, breathing capacity, eyes, and mental alertness were the same as when he was 32 years of age. In his sixties and seventies he beat many of the records he had set in his youth.

Weston had unknowingly tapped into the Upward Spiral of Chi, which is the promise of ChiWalking. In ChiWalking your health and energy can increase as you grow more proficient in your walking and make mindful choices in your life.

Today, many of us have lost sight of walking's potential as a healthy activity and sport. We've been blinded by the glamour of machines, gizmos, and new fitness crazes, forgetting what is right inside us all the time and what is available to us by just getting out the door and taking a walk outside. ChiWalking unlocks the hidden potential in walking by exploring all its vast possibilities. With ChiWalking, you'll get into great physical shape, strengthen your life force, increase your energy, and be inspired for a lifetime.

If I don't limit my enthusiasm for walking, I would say in walking we really have found the Fountain of Youth. Now, that may sound like a ridiculous exaggeration, but I mean it. There are numerous studies that I will cite that show the tremendous health benefits of walking. It truly is a miraculous tonic for your health and well-being.

East Meets West: Maximizing the Benefits of Walking

Walking is the most popular physical activity in the world. In the United States alone, almost 80 million people call themselves walkers; half of these consider themselves "fitness" walkers. It has been shown time and time again that walkers have less incidence of cancer, heart disease, stroke, diabetes, and other killer diseases. Walkers live longer and have a greater optimism about life than those who are sedentary.

Here's a statement that really impressed me in my research on walking: "Research shows that adults who are physically active in their 50s and early 60s are about 35 percent less likely to die in the next eight years than those who are sedentary. For those who have a high heart risk because of diabetes, high blood pressure, or smoking, the reduction is 45 percent." (November 2004 issue of the journal *Medicine and Science in Sports and Exercise*. A study done by researchers at the University of Michigan Medical School and the VA Ann Arbor Health Care System.) The positive effect walking can have in your life is really amazing! It can literally mean the difference between life and death.

There are, however, very few places to learn how to walk correctly. Most people seem to think that walking is like breathing, that we all just naturally walk correctly. Well, first of all, most adults don't breathe correctly (but you'll learn about correct breathing in chapter 3). Second, most people walk in a way that keeps them stuck in poor movement habits that restrict their flow of energy and can even degrade their fitness level.

Also, unlike with breathing, children put a lot of energy and concentration on learning to walk—and they do it really well. Think what joy we all feel at watching a child take her first steps. You'd think she had found the cure for cancer. Well, guess what? She just might have! (There are studies that show that walking reduces the incidence of certain types of cancer.) Yes, toddlers may fall and stumble and look a little like Frankenstein's monster at first, but the makings of perfect walking form are right there. That is, until they start imitating older kids who walk around with "attitude." Kids start changing their posture and walking habits as early as age 4 or 5, when they begin to emulate the movements of us adults who, unfortunately, have picked up some pretty poor habits. We slouch in our chairs, hunch over our desks, cross our legs, stand with our knees locked and our hips thrust forward. Any one of these will cause bones and joints to move in ways that they weren't designed to move.

There are many reasons why we don't naturally walk the way we are supposed to. Through stress and strain, our bodies have become misaligned, imbalanced, and stiff. One place we all tend to hold tension without realizing it is in our pelvic area and hips, the area of our body most involved during walking. Stiffness in our hips translates to the misalignment of the spine and overuse of our legs, which cause injury and fatigue. Most people are walking in a way that often causes back pain, knee pain, foot problems, shin splints, sciatica, and a host of other common ailments. Most men that I observe on the street are walking purely on leg power, holding their pelvis motionless. This overworks their hips and keeps their spine disengaged from their walking. As they age, their hips need to be replaced from overuse and their spine begins to atrophy or disintegrate from the lack of movement. Many of the women I see walking have too little core strength and too much lateral movement in their pelvis. This leads to similar lower-back and hip problems during their later years. Both of these scenarios can be avoided if the right movement habits are established earlier in life.

Take, for example, one of the main premises of ChiWalking, that you lead with your upper body. Watch all people under the age of 4 and you'll see them leading with their upper bodies when they walk. Watch almost all people over the age of 14 and you'll see them leading with their hips and pulling themselves forward with their legs. Believe it or not, our legs are not designed to pull us forward. They are there to move our bodies forward in the world, but they are intended to be powered by our strong center, our engaged core. Your core muscles are those deep muscles that work to stabilize your pelvis during movement. We've all gotten the notion that legs do the walking. No, no, no—our *whole bodies* walk. The power that drives our movement should come from what in Pilates is called the *powerhouse* and what we call in T'ai Chi your *dantien*.

Remember the nursery rhyme "The Farmer in the Dell," about the farmer who takes a wife, who takes a child, who takes a maid? That nursery rhyme explains how things work best on the farm, right down to the mouse taking the cheese. Well, in our current way of walking, we've reversed the way things are meant to be, as if the cheese has taken the rat, who has taken the cat, who has taken the dog, et cetera, ending with the wife taking the farmer who knows where?

In ChiWalking, that nursery rhyme might look something like this:

> *The mind creates the alignment.*
> *The alignment allows the lean.*
> *The lean moves the spine.*
> *The spine moves the pelvis.*
> *The pelvis moves the legs.*
> *And heigh-ho the derry-o, the body moves forward.*

But, instead of the above, here is how many of us are currently walking: our overworked legs push and pull the body forward, our center collapses in weakness, our hips stay locked and inflexible, and our neck and lower back ache because they are twisted out of alignment—*ouch!* What a crazy way to move through life! Now, I am being a bit harsh, but there is a lot of truth in what I am saying. These bad habits can be commonly found in today's walkers. Most people currently walk at about 50 percent efficiency or less. Poor structural alignment and the lack of core muscle strength create a body that is out of balance, inefficient, and often in pain or discomfort.

Many of my clients are interested in completing a walking event because that goal is challenging for them. But walking 5 to 10 miles or a half or full marathon can be daunting. They quickly see that the way they walk causes discomfort, pain, and even injury as they increase the duration of their walks. They are reaching the physical limits of their current walking habits, habits that can hinder their progress and cramp their style.

With ChiWalking, the first step of the Five-Step Process is to get aligned, which means to correct your posture. This alone can counteract many of the problems listed above. You will learn walking habits that increase the flow of energy, open up tight joints, and allow much greater freedom of movement, a freedom that allows you to dream big and reach your goals, whether they are to lose weight, walk a marathon, or just feel great.

THE "CHI" IN CHIWALKING

To create the kind of walking that truly benefits your whole body, you need to start with your mind. Another name for ChiWalking might be "intelligent walking" because in ChiWalking your mind educates your body while your body in turn informs your mind.

ChiWalking is about mastering the sport of walking by turning it into a daily practice from which you will learn efficient movement skills as well as how to direct and transform your energy. Mindful movement along with the free flow of energy through your body will keep you healthy and vibrant for a lifetime and turn your walking into a complete mind-body fitness program.

ChiWalking takes its cues from T'ai Chi, which is based on the study of Nature and the movement of animals. T'ai Chi is an ancient Chinese martial art that has been passed on from one T'ai Chi master to the next over thousands of years. My own teacher, Master George Xu, is world renowned and has learned from the masters of this great lineage. Inherent in T'ai Chi is a deep understanding of the human body and its incredible potential and ability to adapt, change, and learn. At its most elemental, T'ai Chi is the study of energy, chi, or life force. T'ai Chi teaches us that we can cultivate and direct the chi in our bodies by moving our bodies in certain ways, some of them quite simple and yet powerful. By aligning your spine, engaging your core muscles, and relaxing everything else, you tap into an infinite source of chi. It can be as simple as sitting up straight when you find yourself dozing off during a long symphony performance. All of a sudden the fatigue you were experiencing only moments before has vanished, leaving you energized and awake—just in time for the drive home.

In order for chi to flow through your body, you must first open the pathways for it to move freely. Any misalignment in your structure or tightness in your joints and muscles will restrict this flow of energy the same way a crimp in a garden hose restricts water flow. This is where the Five Steps come in. You'll be aligning your posture, engaging your core, and creating balance in your body, which allows chi to flow from the top of your head to your feet. You'll then direct this energy by making a choice and moving forward with this energy.

Additionally, when you are aligned in your body, you also become aligned with the forces of Nature. Gravity becomes your ally, and your body becomes a conduit for the chi in Nature to move through you. When you set up the right conditions for chi to flow—it will.

INTELLIGENT WALKING: THE NEW NORMAL

I enjoy all that walking affords, especially the freedom to explore new places. I also love to challenge myself with more difficult terrain, walking longer distances, and, my personal favorite, seeing how long I can walk without a lapse of focus on following my breath. I did it once for 45 minutes, and it was one of the most memorable walks I've ever had.

Marathon walking has become the goal of millions of people and the new frontier of physical fitness. In a recent poll, more than 70 percent of the walkers surveyed stated a desire to train for and participate in a marathon or other distance-walking event. Almost 38 million Americans identify themselves as fitness walkers. I think the most fascinating frontier for each of us can be the exploration of our own internal self, how we move and what we can do to move more efficiently. We are just scratching the surface of the booming body-mind-spirit connection that everyone talks about. When we learn something deeply and fully through our bodies, it is a gateway to mental and emotional and, yes, even spiritual understandings that can help us evolve and grow as human beings. Those who use yoga or T'ai Chi as a practice understand this. In their quest for human understanding and evolution through movement of the body, yoga's rich, ancient, and spiritual beginnings are similar to those of T'ai Chi.

In ChiWalking we are bringing the knowledge of these ancient traditions into your walking. But don't let that put you off if all this body-mind-spirit stuff does not interest you. If you just want a good fitness program, that's here too, in spades. You can count on it. And that's where we'll focus, on the physical fitness foundation, while giving you information about how these physical practices can have a powerful and wonderful influence on your mental and emotional states.

This Five-Step Process grounds you in very solid physical practices that will allow you to walk healthfully for the rest of your life. That's a big deal. I remember my first T'ai Chi master, Zhu Xilin, talking about what happens when we lose the ability to walk. So much of the aging process really begins to hit home when we're not able to walk as easily and with as much flexibility. Being able to walk with focused, graceful forward movement helps us to move through life with those same qualities—from a place of deep power, knowing where we're going and why. It's simple and yet it works.

None of us should ever take for granted the gift of walking. Through your ChiWalking practice you will be bringing a much-needed mindfulness into the simple act of walking. It presents an opportunity to be respectful of our bodies and respectful in the way we walk through life, if for no other reason than to be a good example for those children who are just taking their first steps. Even you avid walkers can develop a new relationship with walking that allows you to appreciate it more than you ever imagined. It's like being married to someone for years and then learning about a whole new, deeper part of them that you never knew existed—something that makes you fall in love with them all over again.

The difference with ChiWalking is profound. Here are some letters from clients:

I love to walk in the hills and trails around my home, but I was always feeling that it was too much effort. My legs would feel sluggish and worn out from just a short hike. With the help you gave me, I just can't believe the difference it has made. It's as if the hills aren't there anymore, except I still enjoy the views and the beauty. I can go so much further and so much faster than before . . . I'm really enjoying walking again and am so grateful. —*Karen*

I had an amazing experience at mile 18 of my marathon walk. I was getting really tired and my legs were really aching. I dreaded the next 8 miles and was wondering if I shouldn't just stop. I remembered what you said and I really worked on my posture and shortened my stride and leaned forward a bit. At first I didn't think

I was doing it right, but after a short time I found myself moving along and not feeling the tiredness anymore. I didn't realize it at first, but by mile 21 I was feeling great again, energized and ready for the next five miles. I wouldn't say walking the marathon was easy, but I felt pretty great at the end and really thrilled that I'd done it. —*Kevin*

ChiWalking will teach you to walk in balance and with grace and symmetry. From this place you will feel the power and strength in your body, for when you move in balance, tension is minimized and the flow of your chi is maximized. Eventually, moving with a sense of balance and grace will become more than a way of walking—it will become a way of life.

CHAPTER TWO

The Five Mindful Steps

What a piece of work is a man! How noble in reason! how infinite in faculty! in form and moving, how express and admirable! in action, how like an angel! in apprehension, how like a god! the beauty of the world! the paragon of animals!—WILLIAM SHAKESPEARE, *HAMLET* (II, II)

We've created a Five-Step Process to learn the ChiWalking form and to get maximum benefits from your fitness program. In this chapter we'll review each of the Five Steps and how they can get you onto the road to lifelong health and energy. We will apply this process in many different ways throughout the book, and we suggest you use the process in any situation in your life where you need to be attentive to the choices you are making.

Step 1: Get Aligned
Step 2: Engage Your Core
Step 3: Create Balance
Step 4: Make a Choice
Step 5: Move Forward

In ChiWalking, it all starts with getting yourself *aligned*, first in your body, then with your goals. Once your body and mind are aligned, you will *engage your core* muscles. You'll then learn to move in a way that *creates balance*, physically and energetically. From this solid, grounded state of balance you are able to make healthy, informed *choices* and *move forward* in your walking and in your life. Then, as you meet each challenge along your path, you start the process again by checking in with your alignment, engaging your core, and so on. This repeated cycle creates the Upward Spiral of Chi, which leads to a deeper level of stability, increased levels of energy, and a broader, more expansive viewpoint from which to choose your next path or destination.

STEP 1. GET ALIGNED

One of my favorite events to watch in the Olympics is the diving competition. No matter how many flips or twists the top diver makes after leaving the diving board, she always enters the water in the straightest, most streamlined shape possible in order to make the smallest splash. Her arms, spine, and legs are perfectly aligned.

Watch a ballerina as she spins on pointe and you'll see the same body alignment in place. Her spine is straight, and as much of her body as possible is close to her central axis. If she wants to spin faster, she simply pulls her arms or legs in toward her centerline, which immediately accelerates her spin. The bottom line is this: when you're aligned, you're more efficient at what you're doing, whether you're a cyclist, a weight lifter, a grocery clerk, or an opera singer.

In ChiWalking, we begin by aligning our posture as the surest step to creating balance and efficiency in our bodies and in our lives. In T'ai Chi all movement comes from your spine. When your spine is long and tall and straight, chi flows through your spine more easily, just as water flows through a straight pipe much more easily than through a bent pipe.

Throughout this book I will introduce several Chi Principles which come from T'ai Chi and are also the foundation of ChiWalking. These principles are a set of natural laws under which we must all operate. Needle in Cotton is one of these Chi Principles and is at the heart of getting aligned.

NEEDLE IN COTTON: GATHER TO YOUR CENTER AND LET GO OF ALL ELSE

A fundamental principle in ChiWalking that has been taken from T'ai Chi is Needle in Cotton. In the practice of T'ai Chi, all sound movement has this principle at its source. The phrase *needle in cotton* depicts the image of a needle resting in the middle of a ball of cotton. It is an image that a T'ai Chi practitioner should remember while practicing this ancient martial art. The needle represents the thin straight line running vertically through the rotational axis of the body, along the spine. In T'ai Chi, one practices gathering energy (chi) *to* this centerline and initiating all movement *from* this centerline.

In ChiWalking, your spine is the *needle* and your shoulders and arms, hips, and legs are the *cotton*. The more energy you gather in toward your center—your *needle*—the more you must let go of holding any energy in your extremities and imagine them to be as light and airy as *cotton*. If your limbs are tense and rigid, chi cannot flow from your center to your arms and legs and they won't move as easily. Also, any rigidity in your muscles and joints will restrict your range of motion. In ChiWalking you're going to learn to relax the overworked muscles in your hips and legs.

If you want a good visual image to understand the principle of Needle in Cotton, just open up your top-loading washing machine while it's going and watch the motion of the center spindle that is oscillating back and forth. It's rotating on its axis while the water and the clothes are being swished around. The clothes are moved totally at the whim of the spindle and the spindle is offered no resistance by the "fluidity" of the clothes. Try to integrate this image (or whatever one works for you) into your body when you're walking and your gait will take on a whole new sense of fluidity. Always keep in mind that your center is the origin of all your movement and your arms and legs are extensions of your center. In this next section, we'll review *why* alignment is so important. You can practice Needle in Cotton anytime and anywhere. In fact, there is no way you can practice this or any of the other Chi Principles too much, for the same reason that you can't breathe too much clean air—nothing but good will come of it.

PHYSICAL ALIGNMENT

When your posture is straight and your whole structure is aligned, your weight is carried by the sound structure of your bones, ligaments, and tendons rather than by your muscles. We need *some* muscles to hold us up, but with good posture, the bulk of the support work is done by your structure, like the iron pillars of a skyscraper.

We get muscle tension and stiffness when our muscles do the work that our skeleton should be doing. Most backaches come from poor posture and overworked muscles. It is important to align your entire body as well as your spine. When aligning yourself during walking, the best and simplest rule to follow is this: *have as many parts of your body as possible moving in the same direction that you are.* And the best way to ensure that you're within the boundaries of this law is to minimize your side-to-side and up-and-down movements. When walking, it's important to point your arms, legs, and feet in a cohesive forward movement that is aligned with the direction in which you're heading.

When your muscles are freed up from unnecessary work, they can stretch, relax, and move fully, as in a good yoga practice. The number-one issue I find in teaching walking is not poor muscle strength, but muscle tightness and tension that restricts healthy movement. Your muscles will get all the workout they need if they are freed up to move in the way they are meant to. Strong structural alignment gives you the opportunity to move freely, joyfully, and effortlessly.

Having great posture will also increase your lung capacity, allowing you to breathe easier and more deeply. I've had clients who'd swear they had "exercise-induced asthma" when all they really needed to do was learn how to stand up straight and allow oxygen to get deeper into their lungs. We'll cover breathing in chapter 3, "The Chi-Skills."

And the benefits of an aligned body continue, for when you're in alignment you'll not only decrease your odds of getting hurt but also improve your efficiency and your mental clarity.

ENERGETIC ALIGNMENT

If your life (or your walking program) were a movie, your mind would be the director. The director hires the talent and aligns them with the overall feel of the movie. She also decides on the sets, adjusts the lighting, and picks just the right music to further set the tone. It's her job to pull all these elements into *alignment* so that everyone is working toward the same goal. The director has a strong vision for what the movie will look like when it's shown on the big screen and she knows what she needs to make it happen. She's also got to deliver the final product on budget and on time. A good director is both a visionary and a pragmatist.

Your mind, acting as a director, takes the current direction of your life into account and creates your walking program to support that direction accordingly. In chapter 7, you'll assess your goals and abilities and create a walking program that will keep you moving in a healthy direction. You'll start with getting your whole self *aligned* with your vision. When your mind is aligned with your heart and your deepest desires, there is no limit to what can be accomplished. Energetic alignment will ensure the success of any health and fitness program.

Energetic alignment means being clearly and deeply behind what you're doing—willing to dive into whatever is ahead, knowing that every step you take now is one more step in the right direction. It means being willing to be truthful with yourself, realistic in your goals, and able to keep your vision in mind when the going gets tough. Doubts may come up, but with your vision in mind, they'll be more like little tiny voices in the back of your mind, not three-headed monsters that take an army to defeat. Being energetically aligned means knowing what you want and going for it.

ALIGN YOURSELF:
PHYSICALLY AND ENERGETICALLY

Physical alignment gives your *body* more power and energy, and energetic alignment gives *you* more power and energy! Either way, alignment gives you a strong feeling of energy and balance, along with a powerful sense of living from your core.

The ChiWalking technique *aligns* you with the direction you're moving by eliminating extraneous movement. When you make good choices to improve your technique, you become a more efficient *walker*. When you make good mental choices, you become a more efficient *person* by moving in the direction of your intentions and away from mental chaos. This leaves you with a deeper sense of yourself.

STEP 2. ENGAGE YOUR CORE

Can you imagine a tree without a trunk? The strongest part of a tree is right at the base where the roots meet the trunk. The same holds true in your body. The strongest area of your body is your *core*, which supports your trunk just like a tree. When I think of something having a strong core, the first words that come to mind are *power* and *stability*. Your core area is referred to in many different spiritual and cultural traditions as your center. In Pilates, the physical muscles of your abdominal area are referred to as your powerhouse. In Japan, the Samurai called it their *hara*. The Chinese call it their *dantien*. The common thread that runs through all of the various traditions is that they all see the core area of the body as the place where strength and power reside, both physically and energetically. That's why any amount of time spent focusing on this area of your body will increase a sense of self.

In physical terms, your core is responsible for keeping your body vertical and integrated during movement. This is no small thing, which is why it is the most important part of the body to pay attention to. Master Xu is always telling me to relax my shoulders and hips, allowing all of my movement to originate from my center. When I can do that, I find that it's an incredibly efficient way to move my body.

Your core muscles are the muscle group most responsible for stabilizing your pelvis when you stand, walk, or run. They act to hold your spine erect whenever you're in an upright position and they help lift your legs. When your core muscles are weak, it is difficult to stand up straight, and your arms and legs have to work a lot harder whenever you walk or stand or move in any way.

A sense of stability is what we're all searching for, whether it's in our home, in our workplace, on the playing field, or on a ski slope. No one *likes* to feel unstable. Building a stronger core allows you to walk more efficiently and move with more ease. When your central muscles are strong and healthy, the rest of your body doesn't have to work as hard to accomplish physical tasks.

Likewise, on the emotional level, if you have a strong "core," or sense of self, you can move through life's challenges more easily. You'll feel more stable in uncertain situations, like when you're face to face with that rich dessert. In other words, building a strong core physically is one thing, but building a strong internal sense of yourself equates to having willpower when you need it. When you can walk feeling strong and upright, the sense of confidence that it instills will spill over into the rest of your life, and you will begin to experience what "living from your core" means. You'll feel centered in your interactions, intentional in your speech and movement, and grounded in your spirit.

Having willpower means knowing what you want and being able to focus your attention and energy toward that end. Willpower is directly tied to the larger vision you have for yourself. For example, your vision might be to have a strong, healthy body. Where willpower comes in is when life presents challenges to that vision, like being asked by your office mates to go for a pizza just as you are leaving for your daily fitness walk. Your willpower is what says *yes* to your vision and *no* to the pizza as you head out to walk.

When you don't live from your core and from your deeply felt intentions, it is easy to get "swayed" by whatever is outside of you—the latest fad or the shiniest trinket. It was once said, "If you don't stand for something, you'll fall for anything."

People assume that as you age, you should plan on losing some of your ability to stabilize yourself. Falling accounts for over half of the accidental deaths in the elderly. T'ai Chi, yoga, and Pilates are three popular disciplines that have worked to address this problem. There are many core-strengthening exercises that can be done at any age to increase stability and counteract the weakening of the core muscles. Studies have proven that elderly people can greatly improve their balance when they do T'ai Chi regularly. In Chi-Walking you'll be strengthening these very important muscles with every step.

It is very important, however, that your stability is based not on being rigid, but on flexibility. A tree that's too rigid could break in a strong windstorm or under the weight of a heavy snow. I'm always amazed at how stable palm trees look on a quiet day and yet how they can survive hurricane-force winds. Being strong, stable, *and* flexible is what keeps them standing year after year, and the same can hold true for you. A T'ai Chi master remains stable and centered yet mobile and fluid in his response to his attacker.

So when it comes to movement, balance, and general body strength, your core is where it's at. This book will guide you through the process of engaging and strengthening your core so that all of your movement comes from this stable but fluid place.

Since most people have never felt their core working, here's a quick exercise to give you a feeling of what engaging your core does for you. It'll only take a minute. Just stand up, set the book down, and do the following:

- Stand up straight with your feet together.
- Relax the entire abdominal area around your hips and pelvis.
- Now let all of the weight of your body sink onto your left leg. Hold it for a second and then switch support legs by sinking all of your weight onto your right leg.
- Now go back and forth a few times between both legs, alternately resting on one leg and then the other.

You should notice that as you let your weight fall onto each leg your pelvis shifts from side to side, like you're doing a Mae West impersonation.

Now we're going to do the same exercise, but this time you'll engage your core. Here's how:

Stand up straight and level your pelvis by lifting up on your pubic bone with your lower abdominal muscles. Once your pelvis is level, do the same exercise of shifting your weight back and forth between legs. You'll see that your pelvis no longer moves side core is engaged. It's magic!

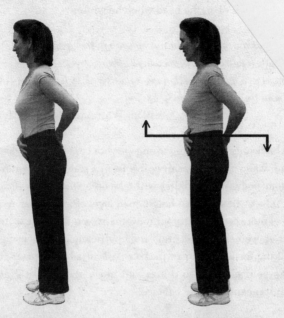

Figure 4a—Core muscles not engaged

Figure 4b—Core muscles engaged, pelvis level

When your core muscles are not engaged, your pelvis has no support and moves from side to side. This lack of support increases the workload on your hips and lower back. If you want to see an example of what it looks like to walk without using your core, watch any model as she walks down the runway at a fashion show. The distinct swish you'll see in her hips lets you know that there's no core involved. You'll never see an Olympic athlete or a ballet dancer walking that way.

When you engage your core, everything else can and should relax. This is important because your core is the home of your chi, from which all your power is emitted. When your core is strong, your arms and legs can relax and become the conduits for all that power to move through your body.

Core strength is connected with inner strength and willpower. A strong core gives you the ability to clearly direct yourself. Walt Whitman hit the nail on the head when he wrote:

> *Sure as the most certain sure, plumb in the uprights,*
> *Well entreatied, braced in the beams,*
> *Stout as a horse, affectionate, haughty, electrical,*
> *I and this mystery, here we stand.*
>
> —Walt Whitman, "Song of Myself"

The beauty of learning to engage your core is that you will begin to stand, walk, and increasingly live from a stable and centered feeling in your body. Your walking will take on a whole new flavor because you'll be walking with a heightened level of awareness. As you begin to feel more centered in your movement, you'll be able to notice when your movement feels tiring and inefficient. Then, using the Chi-Walking focuses, you can make whatever adjustment is required to bring yourself back to center and move ahead with grace. This is what it means to create balance.

STEP 3. CREATE BALANCE

I volunteer in my daughter's Waldorf-inspired kindergarten class every other week. I am so impressed with the teachers, Marianne and Nettie, and the way they create an incredible sense of balance and harmony with twenty-two five-year-olds. From start to finish the day unfolds with a wonderful sense of continuity, purpose, and natural rhythm as the children learn how to work, play, and get along. They teach the kids how to live a well-balanced life by showing that everything has its time and place. There are transitions between activities where they sing songs to remind themselves to look back on what they just did and look forward to what they are about to do. The program includes plenty of time for outdoor activity and quiet time, as well as the use of imagination and development of the mind. The school provides a warm, nourishing snack every day, which my daughter has come to love: rich whole grains such as brown rice, millet, and oatmeal cooked with fruit, nuts, and seeds.

At first glance their day seems simple, but as I look deeper I can see a remarkable testament to the value of balance. There is not too much or too little of anything, and nothing seems to move too quickly or too slowly. These kids are learning a balanced approach to their day that they can carry with them for the rest of their lives. I wish I had gone to a kindergarten like that.

We all deserve to have days that are lived with a sense of purpose, balance, and sanity. But how many of us do? Sometimes it feels like the biggest theme operating in our lives is damage control. Right? ChiWalking has the ingredients for the perfect recipe for creating balance and sanity in your life. With ChiWalking you will also create a fitness program that keeps your body in balance, invigorated, and challenged as well as healthy, vibrant, and fit.

In T'ai Chi and in ChiWalking, creating balance is at the heart of our work. Getting aligned and engaging your core are the means toward the end of creating balance. Physical balance is essential to a sound, efficient walking technique, and a mindful awareness of balance is essential to creating a walking program that truly suits your needs. In life, balance is essential to becoming a whole person.

What is interesting about balance is that it means that there is a center and that things move around that center. You can't create balance without having a center. When your core is engaged, the next step is to create balanced movement around that core. Creating balance is in many respects an ongoing and consistent consciousness of where your center lies.

BALANCED IN YOUR BODY

As always, it is best to start by creating balance on the physical level. When you move yourself forward in balance, your core is doing the majority of the work and the amount of work required of your arms and legs is reduced to a reasonable and proportional amount. The bulk of the work falls to your core muscles. However, sometimes a body is so used to moving in a state of imbalance that it begins to feel

Figure 5a—Walking with stride opening to the rear

Figure 5b—Walking with stride opening to the front

natural and "balanced." However, it's not a truly balanced alignment and it will slowly degrade your health because of so much overcompensation. Here's an example of imbalance: if the top of your body is leaning too far back when you walk, then the legs have to reach forward, which puts undue stress and strain on the legs and lower back. When you use your legs to pull you forward, you're using weaker muscles to do a big job, and you're walking in an unbalanced way. In a truly balanced walk, your body will be moving forward and your legs will be swinging to the rear.

With ChiWalking, we're also going to show you how to create energetic balance in your life through walking. If you're stressed out, we'll show you a walk that will relax you. If you're spaced out and your mind is wandering aimlessly, we'll show you a way to walk that will help you regain focus. When you learn to become aware of your state of imbalance, you can then make a choice to get back to center.

As I mentioned earlier, when you are balanced, both the movement and support of your body require less work. When you're physically out of balance, muscles have to compensate for the lack of balance. For instance, when you stick your neck out, your neck muscles have to work harder to support the weight of your head. When your hips stick too far forward, your glutes and quadriceps have to take over, and the discs in your spine become compressed as well. Triple whammy.

In the ChiWalking form we look for balance and symmetry in many ways. First and foremost, we look to make our body perfectly symmetrical around our core. Take a moment and stand in front of a full-length mirror. Look at the right and left sides of your body. Is one shoulder higher than the other? Does your right foot turn out and your left point forward? Does your head sit squarely on the top of your neck or tilt to one side? Are your hips level? Do both of your arms hang symmetrically at your sides or at different angles? Any asymmetry can cause pain, injury, or just plain more work for you when you walk. As you discover an imbalance, it's important to consciously correct it and bring your body back into balance.

When you are physically balanced, you're not only more efficient in your movement, you're a lot safer moving through life. This becomes especially important for the elderly population, which includes all of us at some point.

BALANCED IN YOUR MIND

When you're mentally and emotionally balanced, you move through life on a more even keel and with less turbulence. You are more able to roll with whatever comes your way, very much as a T'ai Chi master keeps his balance while fighting an opponent. When you're mentally or emotionally out of balance, you pull the plug on your available energy resources. Worrying about the future or obsessing about the past are two ways you can throw yourself off balance from your connection with the present, which is your center. Here's another common example: if you're on a weight-loss program but are obsessed about taking off the weight, you may not eat enough food, which creates an imbalance in how much nourishment you need to take in. This kind of imbalance—lack of needed fuel—will create unhealthy and out-of-balance cravings.

BALANCED IN YOUR PROGRAM

In your walking program it is important to remain balanced in your approach to your workouts. Don't load all your workouts toward the weekend; try to balance the frequency of your walks by spreading them throughout the week. A balanced program would include a variety of walks that give the whole body a healthy workout. It's easy to get overfocused on cardio walks and not balance them with aerobic or loosening walks.

STEP 4. MAKE A CHOICE

Okay, I'll admit it to the world. I was once a *Star Trek: The Next Generation* addict. Even if you're not into *Star Trek,* indulge me for a moment. One of my favorite episodes was when the *Enterprise* (their spaceship) hit a time warp and the ship was split into a million *Enterprises,* each representing various possibilities from one moment in time. One of the characters, Worf, knows something is not right because his reality keeps changing and he gets to see how things would be different if he had made different choices.

When we make a choice in our lives, all the other possibilities dissolve and we move in the direction that our choice takes us. We've all experienced the awareness of making the *big* choices. Whom you marry, which job offer to take, what to study in college. We often lose sight of what a *big* difference the little choices can make in our lives. I would say that the difference between a day *well spent* and a day *just spent* is in the little choices you make all day long. Many of these decisions we make unconsciously, and many are not made from a balanced, aligned place and don't serve us as well as they could.

Hence, Make a Choice comes *after* Get Aligned, Engage Your Core, and Create Balance. Once you have taken the first three steps, you're then ready to Make a Choice. As a matter of fact, whenever you need to make a choice about something in your life, I highly recommend that you take the first three steps on some level—if not physically, then mentally.

In chapter 4, as you get into the ChiWalking form, Make a Choice means that you are going to *choose* to move forward in a new kind of way. In ChiWalking when you move forward you do so by leading with your upper body, *not with your legs.* This is a choice that needs to be made consciously because most people lead with their legs. You will also choose to be focused, or choose to relax your shoulders, or choose to breathe deeply, or whatever it is that you need to work on. But believe me, nothing new will happen unless you make the conscious choice to change what you do.

Making a choice is akin to making a commitment, but not so binding. The point I want to get across in this step is that you are able to make a choice. You can choose to walk six days a week and stick to it. You can choose to train mindfully for a distance event and not get injured or be stiff for days. You can choose to walk mindfully and get the full body-mind benefits of every workout.

Making a choice is the moment before moving forward, when we choose the direction in which we're going to move. It is an absolutely necessary step before you can move forward with conviction.

ChiWalking emphasizes making choices in the moment that best serve your whole body's needs and your whole person's needs. ChiWalking also represents a tool kit of options. No matter what kind of a predicament you're in with your walking program, you have a choice of tools to get you back to center.

Let's say your goal is to walk five days a week to get fit, and tonight is one of your evenings to walk, but you were up late working on a report for work, and one of the kids was up half the night with a cough, and you had a long, hard day at work. You will need to make a choice about what to do.

Rather than make a hasty choice from an out-of-balance place, you can take a few minutes and get back into balance. Start by sitting comfortably in a chair, putting your attention on your body and away from your chaotic thoughts for a few moments to let the day settle (see "Body Sensing," in chapter 3) and to help your mind get clear and focused. You'll then align your posture and breathe deeply (explained in chapter 3), while at the same time remembering your overall vision to get fit. It might take a few minutes, but it is time well spent, for you're now in a much better place to make a clear decision about your evening. You may choose to do a slow, calming walk for about 15 minutes rather than the brisk 40-minute cardiovascular walk you planned. In any case, what matters is that however you choose to move into the evening, it will be a conscious choice, coming from a balanced, centered place. You might even find that at the end of the 15-minute walk, you have discovered that by getting your body moving you tapped into more energy than you thought you had and may choose to continue walking.

We don't realize how many choices we make all day long, many of them very unconscious and decided in an unbalanced state. A common state of imbalance and a common mistake in making a choice is to rely solely on your thought process and not consult with and listen to your body. There is much to be said for the wisdom of your body. Taking the first three steps of this program puts you in a heightened state of awareness about your body and your self. This Five-Step Process is a blueprint for making conscious choices based on the needs of your whole being—your body, mind, and spirit—and not just the ideas in your mind.

It is much easier to create balance in your body than your mind. Unfortunately, most of our bodies are underused and our minds are overused. We have lost trust in the wisdom of body. Here is a great opportunity to quiet the overused mind and put your awareness on your body. What I would like to get across more than anything else in this book is the concept that the best decisions are made when your body is *included* in the process of making a choice. When you practice Chi-Walking on a regular basis, your choices will come from a balanced place because you'll access the data in your mind *and* you'll listen to the counsel of your body. From this place you can move forward with confidence in your chosen direction.

STEP 5. MOVE FORWARD

Once you've got a destination picked out and gathered the tools you'll need for the trip, you're ready to Move Forward. The work of aligning yourself, getting centered by engaging your core, creating balance, and making a choice has been done. Now is the time for action, the time for resolve, and the time to put the pedal to the metal.

Move Forward may seem like the simplest step, but in moving forward, your job is to bring to bear on that movement all the previous steps—and, more important, to continue to move forward in your walk that day, in your walking program for the week, in your quest for lifelong health and energy. In ChiWalking you'll learn a walking form that offers you greater potential to make lifelong health and energy a reality in your life, but it is a process. Move Forward is all about the process, about keeping momentum, about keeping the rhythm going.

When you learn the ChiWalking form in chapter 4, you'll learn about pacing, stride length, and rhythm. I walk with a metronome to keep my pace and rhythm defined, crisp, and on target with my goals. When you choose a walk from the menu of walks in chapter 5, you'll notice they have different cadences. Yes, you can stroll, but to have a high-energy fitness program you'll want to keep yourself moving forward with energy from your core muscles.

To keep things moving forward, we often use the analogy of the soccer ball. To keep a soccer ball moving forward, you need to keep kicking it, strategically, often just gently to keep the ball moving forward ahead of you. In the evenings when Katherine and I are getting tired and our five-year-old is still going strong, we'll often look at each other and say, "Time to kick the ball." We know we have a little ways to go before she's asleep, and we like to give her lots of good energy at the end of the day before bed, but it takes a little oomph, a tap, to keep the energy flowing.

We use this analogy all the time, in our daily work, in writing this book. Kicking the ball keeps things moving forward.

Move Forward also means moving toward your vision and your goals. It means being focused on your destination while being present with the process of getting there. You may create a goal of doing a two-hour hike once a week. You may start out walking four times a week for twenty minutes a day as a starting point. What is essential in ChiWalking is not only that you reach your goal, but also that every step of the process of building up to that two-hour hike is valuable to you and your body. The value comes from the mindful practice of listening to your body and moving your body from an aligned, engaged, balanced place.

In the Upward Spiral of Chi, you keep returning to each step and going through the process repeatedly, creating more and more energy in your life. When the going gets tough, you can regain your energy by returning to step one—check in with your posture, then engage your core once again, check in on your balance, and then choose what to focus on next. These steps will keep you moving forward in a healthy, energizing way.

With the ChiWalking program you'll have all the tools you need to create an invigorating and challenging walking fitness program that can help you achieve whatever goal you choose. You'll learn to move in a way that is in harmony with the way you are meant to move and fully supported by the laws of Nature. The Upward Spiral of Chi is a tool that you can use over and over, for any endeavor, at any level. For your ChiWalking program the Upward Spiral of Chi is a step-by-step tool to help you arrive safe, healthy, and vibrant at the destination of your choice.

The good news is that it's not difficult to change. Yes, you do have to be mindful—that is why the book is subtitled *Five Mindful Steps*. You do have to *make a choice* and *move forward* with the choice you have made. You have to engage your will and use your brain. All I can say is, it's worth every step. The changes you will feel in your body (and yes, your mind and spirit) when you're moving as you are meant to will be pretty wonderful—even potentially *really* wonderful.

CHAPTER THREE

The Chi-Skills

Make every move count.
Pick your target and hit it.
Perfect concentration means
Effortless flowing.
—DENG MING-DAO, *365 TAO DAILY MEDITATIONS*

We needed part of our house painted recently. Two bedrooms, a bath, and a hallway all needed some much-deserved TLC. Frank, our neighbor who lives a couple of doors down from us, is a high-end housepainter who's practiced his craft for thirty years, painting everything from old Victorians in San Francisco to mansions in Mill Valley. Needless to say, he's impeccable at his work and *really* fast. He's done painting in just about every house in our neighborhood, so we asked him if he'd do our little job. Painting is an intermittent house chore that I usually do, but it is neither my favorite pastime nor one of my best skills (as Katherine will attest). So I was happy to relinquish my responsibility to master Frank. I say "master" with deepest respect after watching him work his trade. He was nothing short of amazing. I felt like I was witnessing a Japanese tea ceremony, where there wasn't a single move that was out of place. His every movement was so methodical and precise, there wasn't a wasted motion in his entire workday. There were none of the usual splatters and drips that plague my painting. The paint on his brushes never went more than halfway up the bristles, so they came clean in seconds at the end of the day. When he was doing detail work around doors and outlets, his brushstrokes were perfectly straight and done in one pass. His stepladder was always in the perfect spot for the best reach. There were special holders and hooks keeping all of the smaller tools and brushes within an arm's reach. He was truly beautiful to watch because he was a master of his movement and his tools.

Walking is just like painting, because tools and technique play a crucial role in the quality of the outcome. This chapter is about mastering the tools of graceful movement and learning the skills that will turn your walking program into an engaging practice that will last a lifetime. These are life skills that you'll be practicing while you're walking, but their use is not limited to walking. They're a basic set of skills for engaging anything on a deeper level. The Chi-Skills have a broad range of applications. In terms of your body, you'll walk more efficiently and gracefully. And in terms of your mind, you'll expand your walking from an exercise routine for your body to a mindful practice for your own personal growth. This set of skills will form the foundation of your approach to walking and allow you to learn and practice the ChiWalking technique with confidence and clarity.

Here are the five Chi-Skills:

1. Focusing
2. Body Sensing
3. Flexibility
4. Breathing
5. Consistency

These Chi-Skills are unique in that they contain both the process and the goal. For example, the more you focus your mind (process), the more you become a focused person (goal). Likewise, if every time you go out for a walk you focus on being flexible (process), you'll become a more flexible person (goal). Just take a second and imagine what you would be like if you were focused *and* flexible. You might not recognize yourself.

1. FOCUSING

The ability to have a focused mind is a tremendous asset in life. The most successful people have the strongest ability to focus their minds on their long-term goal and on the task at hand. Focus keeps you on a direct path to your goal. Just like a river needs its banks to keep it flowing, your mind needs focus to keep it from wandering and straying from your desired intention.

In chapter 4 you will get the specific instructions to learn the Chi-Walking form. Each instruction is called a Form Focus, because each is a specific instruction you focus on to improve your walking. Focuses have been used for millennia as a way to narrow down the wanderings of the mind to bring oneself into the moment. In a meditation practice a focus could be gazing at a candle or simply watching your breath. In golf, it's keeping your eye on the ball. In ChiWalking you focus on directing and listening to your body.

Let's say, for instance, that the Form Focus is *relaxing your shoulders*. Your mind would then put its attention on your shoulders to see whether they are relaxed. If your mind senses tension, it will direct your arms to swing a little more loosely, then it will watch to see whether or not the instruction worked. If it did, great! If it didn't, your mind might try something else, like directing your arms to hang limp at your sides. Then it would monitor the response and so on. There's always a mental and a physical component to a Form Focus.

Focusing your mind exercises the brain. In ChiWalking, your mind gets a workout by scanning your body, then by directing the body with a Form Focus and then listening to the response. It tells your body when to work and when to relax. There are times when your mind *will* wander, and rather than focus on your body and the movements you'll be practicing, you'll start to think about something else, such as the project you have due at work, the disagreement you had with your coworker, the menu for your upcoming dinner party. It *will* wander. Your job, the exercise that you will give to that wandering mind, is to come back to your Form Focus as often as possible. When your mind wanders, you will refocus it on your movement. Every time you refocus, you're building your mind's muscles. So your job is not to *stay* focused, because you won't for very long, but to *refocus* your mind over and over. We suggest using a watch that has a beeper. You can use the beeper as a tool to refocus your mind. You can set it to repeat in 1-minute intervals. You will think of a Form Focus, such as lifting your heels. For as long as you can, your mind will direct your heels to be lifted up in the back, and your mind will monitor how well your body is doing. Then your mind will wander to that new pair of shoes you saw in the store, or your child's bicycle tire that needs air, and your beeper will go off—ahhh, yes, back to the Form Focus. You may find your heels are still lifting, that your body learned this new Form Focus easily, or that you need to repeat this Focus for 5 or 10 more minutes to really get it right.

PRACTICING MINDFULNESS

Learning to focus your mind during ChiWalking will sharpen your mind's eye. It takes practice, but eventually you'll become adept at watching your actions, not only while walking, but all through your day. Being observant of your actions is called mindfulness, and it is one of the oldest practices on earth. Being mindful in our daily activities brings a whole new level of richness to life. When we're not consumed with thoughts of the past and worries of the future, we can be present in the moment with whatever is in front of us. Everyone always says how envious they are of children, because they can be so "in the present." Younger children are indeed very much in the present, but they're not mindful and they're not supposed to be. As conscious adults, it is our "work" to regain the presence of a child while also being mindful in the moment.

The interesting thing about the mind is that focusing it actually allows it to rest because it is not thinking of a hundred things at once. That's why meditation quiets and rests the mind. When you can narrow your thoughts down to just a few, it really gives your brain a break from the chaos. Then, when you come back into your everyday life, you can function more clearly. Focusing the mind has the incredible dual role of both strengthening and resting the mind at the same time. How's that for multitasking?

The ChiWalking focuses act to engage the mind repeatedly, which strengthens its ability to focus. If you want to build a stronger muscle in your body, you find a specific exercise that works to strengthen that particular muscle. Then you repeat the exercise regularly until the muscle becomes strong. Your mind works in much the same way. If you want to train your mind to work better, engaging it repeatedly with a single focus will do the trick.

I've heard that the average human uses about 10 percent of his or her brain capacity. I think that number is generous. Our minds wander so much during the day that it's amazing we get anything done. Learning to focus your mind with ChiWalking will enable you to return to your center, to alignment, and to balance. With a focused mind you'll become adept at observing your actions and sensing your body, and more mindful of how you move through life. This is the promise of ChiWalking: to build a strong mind and body and the connection between them.

2. Body Sensing

Body Sensing is the act of observing and feeling your body—listening to what it is telling you. Almost everyone I know has a body. It's an unavoidable requirement for participating in life. And since the body is our main vehicle for experiencing life, you'd think that we would give it a pretty high priority when it comes to taking good care of it. Correct me if I'm wrong, but there are people who take better care of their *cars* than they do of their bodies. Every day we read about people doing incredible things with their bodies, from climbing Mount Everest without oxygen, to walking a marathon, to having a baby. Unfortunately, we also read about the incredible amount of abuse that people carry out on themselves, from shooting up drugs to working a seventy-hour week. What I'm getting at here is that we all need to learn the importance of taking good care of ourselves. And where it starts is learning how to sense whether or not what we're doing to ourselves is healthy, in both the long and short term. Body Sensing is the tool for making wise lifestyle choices, and it can be learned and mastered by anyone wishing to develop a clear link of communication between the mind and the body.

Think of your mind and body as a married couple, lifelong partners working together for the higher good of the whole. Body Sensing trains your mind to deeply listen to your body, paying close attention to the sensations, feelings, and impulses that float in and out of your consciousness during your waking hours. One partner—your body—senses and feels what is going on each moment, while the other partner—your mind—observes, collects data, and responds appropriately.

Eckhart Tolle, author of *The Power of Now*, says, "If you keep your attention in the body as much as possible, you will be anchored in the Now. You won't lose yourself in the external world, and you won't lose yourself in your mind. Thoughts and emotions, fears and desires, may still be there to some extent, but they won't take you over."

YOUR BODY IS ALWAYS TALKING TO YOU

Your body is *always* talking: "There's an itch on my leg . . . neck is tense . . . shoulders hurt . . . feet are cold . . . shoes are tight . . . stomach is full." It's an endless conversation that begins when you wake up in the morning and doesn't stop until you're back in bed at the end of the day, headed for dreamland. Considering the sheer amount of information our bodies try to convey to us, it's incredible how little time we actually take to listen. The body has an awful lot to say and the less we listen to it *now*, the louder it will scream later—through injury, illness, or dysfunction. All those little aches and pains in my body are trying to tell me that there's something not right with what I'm doing.

Have you noticed how often we are bombarded with ads for products specifically designed to keep us from feeling what it is that we're doing to ourselves? I recently read an ad for an over-the-counter pain reliever that went something like "When my body is talking pain . . . I try to keep the conversation short." Well, it seems to me that if my body is complaining, I owe it to myself to figure out what I'm doing to cause the complaint and make the necessary adjustments to address it.

For example, a stomachache could be telling you any one of the following things:

- What you ate wasn't good for you.
- You didn't chew your food well enough.
- You ate too much.
- You're worrying too much.
- You're hungry.
- Your belt is too tight.

The following three steps will help you learn the skill of Body Sensing. Whenever you're working with a Form Focus, these steps will help you to ascertain your effectiveness.

Listen Carefully

The first step in Body Sensing is to learn to simply listen to your body without the idea of changing anything—just observing how your body feels when you're either moving or stationary. Pretend you're a detective and you're just gathering information. When you're walking, ask yourself what feelings or sensations are happening inside you. There's no need to judge what you sense and there's no need to correct anything that feels improper. Just listen and observe, listen and observe.

Assess the Information

Once you get good at feeling sensations in your body, you will learn to assess the information that you've gathered. If you're practicing a Form Focus, for instance, you'll be sensing its effect on your movement. Is it helping? Does it make movement easier or more difficult? Does it create a different sensation in your body? Are you moving more freely, faster, slower? What feels right? Is there more or less discomfort?

Adjust Incrementally

If, after assessing your sensations, you feel that an adjustment is necessary, be sure to make it small and incremental. In this way, you'll be less likely to overadjust and go past the "sweet spot" where your Form Focus works optimally.

The three steps of Body Sensing allow you to trace your sensations to their origin, evaluate them, and then make any necessary adjustments. Here are two scenarios of how the process might work. Let's say the weather is hot for a number of days and you forget to drink enough water. You begin to feel a little dehydrated, but you're so busy that you don't make the immediate attempt to get to the water cooler for some water. The next morning you wake up with a slight sore throat so you pop in a throat lozenge to make it feel better, which it does, and you forget about your sore throat until the next morning, when you wake up with a head cold and you can't figure out where it came from. So then you take some sort of cold medicine to keep your nose from running like a faucet and you basically "wait out" the cold until it goes away. But instead of going away, it turns into a sinus infection. By this time you've missed a couple of days of work along with that great art exhibit that you've been waiting months to see.

Now trace back the scenario to the hot weather. If you had been Body Sensing, you might have noticed that the weather was rather warm and that you were sweating a little more than normal. From sensing that, you might have had the intention of drinking a little more water than usual to keep up with your increased rate of perspiration. Had you followed that first sensation of being warm and thirsty and responded with the adjustment of drinking more water, you might not have gone through the entire scenario of getting dehydrated and ending up sick. And, as it turns out, all those cold medicines you took weren't really doing you any favors either. They were actually suppressing the symptoms that were warning of things to come. Sound familiar? Ending up with aches and pains in your body or having a chronic illness is no accident and should come as no surprise if you have ignored what your body was trying to tell you all along the way.

Two of the main things that I'm doing when I'm walking are listening to my body and making adjustments. *Neutral vigilance* is the key phrase here. It's important to stay as neutral as possible because we sometimes have the tendency to *exaggerate* what we perceive our sensations to be. When that happens, a small knee pain can rule your world, or the just the *thought* of walking 10 miles could leave you exhausted.

While I'm out walking, I'm constantly monitoring my body and watching for anything that might need my attention. If I find anything that needs my attention, I'll make an adjustment and then listen for a response from my body to see if the adjustment did any good. It's a constant back-and-forth conversation between my mind and my body, with the ongoing intention of listening and responding. All of the ChiWalking focuses will serve to help you to become aware of what your body is doing. They're also there to help you to learn to direct your body to move in a way that is smoother and more energy efficient. Here's an exercise that I highly recommend for you to learn to Body Sense:

The Body Scan

Here's an exercise you can do while you're walking to help you practice Body Sensing. Remember, it's just an exercise in learning to *observe* your body and is only the first step in learning to Body Sense. It's not necessary to make any adjustments, just watch.

The next time you go out for a walk, do this. Once you're warmed up and well into your walk, begin by putting your focus at the top of your head and slowly scan yourself from head to toe observing any sensations that you meet along the way. Stop at each location for a few seconds and then move on from area to area making mental notes of what you find along the way. Move from your head to your neck . . . then to your shoulders . . . arms . . . chest . . . abdomen . . . lower back . . . pelvis . . . hips . . . upper legs . . . knees . . . lower legs . . . ankles . . . and finally feet and toes. It helps to do this Body Sweep at least once during every walk and is best if you can do it more often than that, like when you're sitting at your desk or driving your car.

Here are some questions you might ask yourself: Do I feel tension here? Relaxed here? Heavy, light, soft, open? Get the idea? Just watch and observe and see which descriptions come to mind. Here's a tip: the more you watch, the more you'll see. All of this observation will eventually give you a great base from which to respond with the correct action.

You can never know your body too well. It is a great and wonderfully mysterious thing, and by making the effort to sense what it's telling you, you can use it as your guide to learning how to move through your life in a healthy and vibrant way.

3. FLEXIBILITY

I once heard someone say that we are the most perfectly designed organism in the universe. That seemed like a tall statement at the time, so I asked her to elaborate, and here's the gist of what she told me. We are incredibly mobile because of our two legs. We can easily move in all directions. We can run, jump, stand upright, and sit. We have two arms with lots of fingers to pick up and hold things, small and large. We have two eyes that are set apart which give us the luxury of depth perception. And then there is our brain, which can do complex thinking and figuring. All of these attributes make us an adaptable species. We've even spent time on the moon.

This body of ours was "designed" to perform in a myriad of activities and situations. In short, we're meant to be variable, to change. Being static is not in our nature. We're meant to evolve and develop at a much higher rate than all of the other plants and animals that occupy this planet. For all of these reasons, flexibility is one of the basic Chi-Skills. Adaptability is a form of flexibility, and the more flexible you are, the more quickly you'll be able to handle whatever comes your way, from the road or from life.

Good health is dependent on the ability of chi to flow through your body, because all of our vital organs are reliant on the circulation of chi to function optimally. Any tightness or restriction in movement will limit this flow, leaving you vulnerable to disease. In Chinese medicine most ailments and diseases are attributed to the lack of free-flowing chi. When your muscles, ligaments, and tendons are relaxed and flexible, blood, oxygen, and chi can flow more easily through your system, making exercise much easier on your heart, lungs, and your body in general. Flexibility also plays a major role in injury prevention, because pulled muscles and tendons are by far the dominant type of exercise-related injury and are caused by tension and tightness.

FLEXIBILITY: USE IT OR LOSE IT

One of the biggest things we have going for us as kids is our flexibility, and I don't mean only physical flexibility. Our bodies and nervous systems are supple when we're infants so that we can better absorb the "shock" of this new plane of existence, moving from the safety of the womb into the comparatively harsh reality of life. Sometime in early adulthood, we begin to restrict our movement. For example, in *Reviving Ophelia*, Mary Pipher talks about how adolescent girls begin to restrict themselves physically and mentally to conform to peer pressure and social restrictions. I see it at the pool we go to. One year the girls are playing as vigorously and wildly as the boys, and the next year, they are self-consciously sitting by the pool, while the boys their age are still as active as ever. Eventually self-consciousness afflicts the boys too and restricts the flow of their energy.

As we age, our hips and knees don't seem to work as well as they used to, and it seems more difficult to accomplish things we once took for granted, such as climbing a tree or tying a shoe. If you are physically inflexible, you're more likely to become mentally inflexible as you age and vice versa. When you can't move as easily, you don't take as many chances and you begin to limit the "range of motion" in your mind.

How do you break out of this pattern? Movement is the key. If you want to remain open to new ideas, you need to be flexible in your thinking. If you want to experience the flow of energy in life, you must have a certain amount of flexibility in your body.

Examples of flexibility, or the lack thereof, can be seen everywhere. A tree that is flexible is less likely to be broken in a storm. If you're uptight when talking with a child, he will sense it and become a perfect mirror of your rigidity. When two warring governments are having peace talks there is always a need, on the part of both sides, to show flexibility and restraint. In T'ai Chi, if you're not flexible and relaxed, you won't be as quick when responding to an attack. Just think: an inflexible snake would only be able to move in one direction for its entire life!

FLEXIBILITY IN LIFE

Remember the principle of Needle in Cotton from chapter 2? In order to be effective in T'ai Chi, or in life, one needs to have a core that is strong as steel, while at the same time maintaining an exterior that is as soft as cotton. In other words, strive to be guided by your core beliefs, yet be flexible in how you meet the outside world.

For instance, when you're out and about, focusing on a specific part of your walking technique, you'll learn to keep centered no matter what kind of terrain you're walking through. That's the *steel.* The *cotton* aspect of this is to respond to the terrain with flexible joints and muscles that can handle any conditions, like walking up and down hills or along winding trails. A great image to think of is a stalk of bamboo, which is incredibly strong yet flexible and resilient.

In chapter 6 we will talk about flexibility and stretching both during and after your walks. Integrating a consistent amount of stretching into your daily regimen is not only strongly suggested, I call it your ticket to longevity. In China, T'ai Chi and Chi Gung are widely accepted as practices that promote health and longevity through mental focus and flexibility. Yoga and Pilates are two conditioning systems that have made great inroads into the health scene of America's baby boomers by promoting flexibility. Both are centered around keeping the muscles, ligaments, and tendons healthy, supple, and strong, all of which promotes good balance and mobility at any age. But as valuable as they are for promoting health, neither is a weight-bearing form of exercise. If you could take your yoga out on your walks with you, would it increase the quality of your walks? You bet! ChiWalking takes the best principles of T'ai Chi, yoga, and Pilates and uses them to promote the flexibility of your joints, ligaments, and tendons while walking.

Over the years, as Katherine and I have developed the ChiWalking Menu you'll find in chapter 5, we've really enjoyed experimenting and playing with all the possibilities that walking offers. You can do the same thing. In ChiWalking, the increased flexibility of your mind and your body gives you greater options in your walking and in your life. When you get flexible and loose, the creativity and spontaneity that are unleashed may surprise you!

4. BREATHING

Proper breathing can energize, calm, cleanse, or empower the body as well as the mind. Breathing is such an important topic because, hey, when it stops, you're history. So, working with your breath will naturally play a big part in your walking practice. In many spiritual practices, breathing is the pathway to deeper states of relaxation, mental alertness, and heightened consciousness.

Breathing happens automatically, but breathing correctly is a learned skill. I can say that because the vast majority of people I've taught over the years didn't know how to breathe deeply or efficiently, and let's face it, most people don't give breathing a second thought. It's so automatic that it even keeps going when you sleep. However, just because you breathe automatically doesn't mean that you're breathing correctly or providing your body with all the oxygen it needs. As with walking, most people think that because they breathe all the time, it is not something they need to learn or practice. The opposite is true. Since breathing and walking are such regular, everyday parts of your life, the better you do them, the more positively they can impact your life.

The biggest problem I see with people who complain about being short of breath during exercise is that they aren't getting enough air into their lungs. Shallow breathing is the culprit. If your lungs remain full of air between breaths, there will be less oxygen exchange with each inhalation. In most cases, having a shortness of breath isn't because you're not breathing *in* enough—it's because you're not breathing *out* enough. If you don't empty your lungs fully with each exhale, you'll be "recycling" some of the carbon dioxide left in your lungs from the previous breath, which will lower the concentration of oxygen getting to your muscles.

Emptying your lungs fully will create a vacuum into which fresh air can enter. If your breath is shallow, each new breath is met with a large amount of old air that will inhibit the "new air" from getting to the lower lungs. It's a scientific fact that if you breathe only into the upper part of your lungs, you're getting only a fraction of the air that you could be because there are relatively few alveoli (those little sacs in your lungs that exchange air/oxygen for blood/oxygen) in your upper lungs. Most of the air exchange happens deeper down in your lungs. So in order to get air further down, you'll need to learn how to clear out the old air by *belly breathing*, just as in yoga class.

The people I see breathing correctly are usually not old enough to read this book. Watch a child's breath while she's sleeping. If she's lying on her back, the only movement you'll see will be her belly rising and falling with each breath. We all started out breathing this way, but most of us have lost the ability to breathe as we did when we were children. Tension and poor posture are just a couple of the reasons why adults don't breathe as deeply as we once did. Once you learn how to "go back" to belly breathing, you'll be able to breathe easily for the rest of your life.

Belly Breathing

Have you ever tried to clear the smoke out of your kitchen after totally burning your dinner? If you have, you know that if you put a fan in the kitchen window to blow fresh air *into* the room, it takes forever to clear the smoke. A better way to exhaust the smoke is to turn the fan around and blow the smoke *out* of the room. Right? By doing this, the outgoing smoke is quickly displaced by incoming fresh air and your smoke-filled kitchen will be back to normal *way* before the pizza guy shows up. It works the same way with your lungs. If you want to get fresh air in, you have to blow the bad air out first.

Here's how to belly breathe:

- Start by straightening your posture. If your upper body is rounded or collapsed forward, it could reduce your lung capacity by up to 30 percent. Stand straight and tall, but don't tense any muscles to do it.

- Place one hand over your belly button.
- Purse your lips like you're trying to blow out a candle and when you exhale, pull your belly button in toward your spine by contracting your abs. Use your hand to feel this motion. This will force all of the used air out of the bottom of your lungs.
- When your inhale is complete, simply relax your abs, letting your lower lungs fill as your stomach returns to its natural position.
- Once your lower lungs are filled to capacity, let your intercostals (the muscles between your ribs) expand to fill the remainder of your lungs.
- When you exhale, relax your chest first, then pull in your belly button and repeat the pattern.

There is really no better way to get more oxygen into your lungs, especially during exercise.

SHORTNESS OF BREATH

If you experience shortness of breath while walking, you might be doing something else besides breathing shallowly. Here are a few possibilities:

You Might Have a Low Aerobic Capacity

This means that your muscles do not have enough capillary beds in place to keep up with the demand for oxygen during exercise. This is absolutely *normal* for those who are just beginning an exercise program after a period of low physical activity. The best way to build aerobic capacity is to exercise moderately for longer periods of time. You don't need to raise the level of intensity (that's cardiovascular exercise). You just need to walk at a sustained medium-effort level (aerobic exercise). If you judge your effort on a scale of 1 to 10, 1 being very casual and 10 being as fast as you can go, you should be at about 5 or 6. The more often you walk and the longer you walk, the more your aerobic capacity will improve.

You Might Have a Low Lung Capacity

This is pretty easy to fix. Just keep your upper body fully extended when you walk. Practice the posture exercise in chapter 4. Working to straighten your upper spine does wonders for your breathing. If you're collapsed forward or round-shouldered, you'll have much more difficulty getting a full breath. One of my clients, who is a voice teacher, assured me that good posture is crucial for maintaining a strong voice because the lungs can fill more fully between breaths.

You Might Be Carrying Tension in Your Muscles

You're not alone here. We all hold tension in our muscles to some extent—some more than others—and it actually does serve a very positive function. It provides a continual source of income for all of those hardworking massage therapists out there. My T'ai Chi teacher is constantly tapping me on the shoulders to remind me to stop holding tension there. He says that when my muscles are tense, I'm restricting the flow of Chi through my body. Oops! Busted again.

I cannot emphasize enough the importance of deep breathing. Here's another interesting tidbit. When your cells are starved of oxygen, free radicals are formed, and these contribute to cell destruction. This is no small matter. To put it in terms that hit home, free radicals are major contributors to premature aging and age-related maladies such as cancer, atherosclerosis, emphysema, cataracts, glaucoma, high blood pressure, immune-system deficiencies, heart disease, arthritis, stroke, Parkinson's disease, various skin disorders, and wrinkled skin. In *Dynamic Nutrition for Maximum Performance,* authors Daniel Gastelu and Dr. Fred Hatfield say, "A high-oxygen diet [breathing more deeply] yields maximum amounts of biological energy with minimum production of toxic waste products and free radicals."

Now, doesn't that make you want to pay a little more attention to how well you breathe?

The practice of watching one's breath is called *mindful breathing* because you are attempting to be mindful of each breath as a way to focus your mind and pull it away from being scattered. In chapter 5 we'll show you how to do a walking meditation that will involve using your breath to calm and focus your mind. There are also breathing techniques that can increase your mental alertness, which we will also discuss.

Thich Nhat Hanh, a famous Vietnamese Zen master, has written volumes about breathing and meditation. In *The Miracle of Mindfulness* he says, "Breath is the bridge which connects life to consciousness, which unites your body to your thoughts . . . To master our breath is to be in control of our bodies and our minds."

In ChiWalking, breathing is a Chi-Skill that you'll work with in all your walks and that has a big impact on your lifelong health and energy. By breathing correctly you'll maximize the energy you gain from every walk, from all that you do, and with every breath. When you're in touch with your breath, you're more in the present, and that's where real choice happens.

5. CONSISTENCY

When you see the Grand Canyon, you cannot help but be in awe of the grandeur and beauty, and of the fact that it was all created by the consistent flow of a river. Likewise, the best athletes in the world are the ones who blow our minds with their ability to perform consistently at a seemingly miraculous level. That doesn't happen by chance. It comes from repeated, ongoing, persistent effort applied over time.

Just as the consistency of your breath or your heartbeat keeps you alive year in and year out, staying consistent with your fitness program will keep you continually in great shape. I've mentioned that practicing the ChiWalking focuses will not only upgrade your walking, but will spill over into your life as well. Consistently practicing your focuses every time you go out for a walk is what makes the "spillover" happen. You'll be so used to remembering the focuses that you'll find yourself thinking about them when you're out running errands. The more consistently you can stay with your walking program and practice the ChiWalking focuses, the more easily you'll remember to engage them at other times. You might find yourself practicing your posture while standing in line at the grocery store, or leveling your pelvis while you're driving your car, or centering yourself before walking into your boss's office to ask for a raise.

The number-one reason why people stop walking—and stop benefiting from all the life-saving, weight-reducing, cardiovascular, stress-reducing, and mind-clearing effects—is that they lack consistency in their walking program. In fact, consistency is the cornerstone of any successful program, from AA to weight loss to raising a child.

MAKING WALKING A PRACTICE

This brings up the question of the century: How do you achieve and maintain consistency in your walking program, year in and year out?

Allow it to occupy a place of stature *equal* with all the other important activities in your life. As difficult as that might seem, here's how you can do it. Make it a *practice*. That's right. Turn your walking into a vehicle for personal growth as well as for fitness. This will add a higher level of integrity and intention to your approach because you'll find that it is a way to deepen and upgrade your relationship to your body. Instead of merely giving your legs a good workout, you'll be practicing to relax more, to breathe better, to expand your vision, to open up your range of motion, to increase your energy, to feel and sense your body. The list is exciting—and endless. With all of this to look forward to, your walking program will take its place alongside everything in your life you value most, and you'll be amazed at how easy it is to schedule time for something you really love to do.

The following quote really strikes to the heart of what a truly mindful practice is:

Build your life brick upon brick.
Live a life of truth,
And you will look back on a life of truth.
Live a life of fantasy,
And you will look back on delusion.
　　　　　　　—Deng Ming-Dao, *365 Daily Tao Meditations*

What is a *practice*? It is a regular, mindful activity that works to enhance your quality of life. It's something you work at every day. A truly good practice will help your body, emotions, mind, and spirit to evolve and progress. You can practice any activity, but making that particular activity a practice elevates it to a much higher level of importance and fulfillment.

When I think about what it means to make my walking a "practice," it becomes much more than just repeating an activity to perfect a skill. I want to be able to use my walking not only to keep my body in good physical shape, but also to learn where I'm not able to flow in my movement, or as a vehicle to learn about life, or to gain a regular helping of the chi that is so abundant in Nature. Your walking then becomes much more than just a fitness activity. It will become a combination of best friend, mentor, teacher, and inner guide. The practice is to be a good listener, a good student, and a good practitioner of what you learn. Here are some tips for how to make walking a practice:

- Be consistent. Know exactly which days of the week and what times you're going to walk. Stay with the program. This will teach you to be persistent and precise (chapter 7).
- Know which focuses you are going to be using during your walks. This will help to improve your mind-body connection and to develop the practice of mindfulness (chapter 5).
- When you finish your walk, spend a few minutes to do an "end-of-walk review." Look back to see how well you did with keeping your focuses, how your body felt during the walk, what you learned. Look for anything that you can come away with that will help you in the future. Then the next time you go out for a walk, you'll have something to work with that you brought forward from your last walk. In this way, your walking program will begin to establish a continuum rather than become a series of random acts (chapter 6).
- Do everything in your ChiWalking program with *qualitative exactitude*. That's a mouthful, but it means to do things with the **highest quality** you can muster. First, be sure you're clear with each focus you're about to do, and then be as precise as possible

when you're carrying it out. When you engage your program with this high level of focus and attention, you'll be amazed at how quickly and powerfully results will come. For instance, if you're working on straightening up your posture, don't just *sort of* work on your posture. Be meticulous in your practice. Don't miss a detail. Be precise now and you'll build the habit of having *great* posture instead of just pretty good posture.

A practice is *process* oriented. It is not about reaching a specific goal, although I encourage you to have goals. It is even more important that the practice continues after the goal is reached and that you enjoy the richness of the process that gets you there.

More Tips on Being Consistent

Here are some great ways to stay consistent with your ChiWalking program:

- **Give your walking a high priority.** Schedule your walking into your life as you would an important business meeting—write it down on your calendar and honor that time as you would a meeting with your boss. Second, create a walking program that is reasonable and keeps your walking fun. By "reasonable," I mean what is actually doable. Don't try to walk 30 miles a week when you only have time to train for 15 miles.
- **Don't be repetitious.** It's easy to make your walking program more fun. Mix it up a little by walking in new places, and make sure you try a variety of the walks in the ChiWalking Menu in chapter 5.
- **Have walking dates.** Make a regular scheduled walking date with a friend. Having company on a walk always makes the time fly by.
- **Don't be afraid of the weather.** Cold and wet outside? Don't let that stop you. Walking in the cold and wet may not feel great for the first few minutes, but as we all know, you get pretty warm walking, and with good gear you can stay reasonably dry. It can be very invigorating to walk in the rain stomping through puddles like a kid. Hey, if Gene Kelly could do it . . .

- **Don't limit the time of day when you walk.** Dark mornings and evenings got you down? Walking in the dark can be an adventure (again, if you have the right gear including plenty of light reflectors so you'll be visible). Even in winter weather you can enjoy being outdoors and feel quite alive, outside in the elements. Always walk in well-lit places and with a partner.
- **Walk after meals, especially big ones.** It is easy to get distracted and forget about taking care of ourselves, especially around vacations and holidays. These are the times when it is difficult at best to keep a solid rate and rhythm going. I've found it best to commit myself to a good, brisk walk after each meal. It is the quickest, best way to get great exercise, breathe some fresh air, take a break from the festivities, and counteract some of my favorite indulgences.

As you create consistency in your walking practice, your body gets accustomed to doing a given activity at a specific time of day. This builds a sense of rhythm into your life that is regular and dependable.

Having consistency in your program also makes it way easier to get back on the horse if you happen to fall off. A program that runs like clockwork takes on a momentum of its own and makes it harder for small setbacks to become big ones. The more earnestly you dedicate yourself to being consistent with your program on a daily and weekly basis, the more it'll be there for you when you need it most.

Approach your program as if you were tapping a soccer ball to keep it moving. If you let it come to a stop between kicks, it will take much more force to get it rolling again. But if you just tap the ball gently each time it slows down, maintaining a good momentum will seem effortless.

The five Chi-Skills are actually commonly used skills that we all take for granted but which can show you how to engage your life in a deeper way. When you practice these skills on a regular basis, you can take any ordinary activity, such as walking, and transform it into something extraordinary.

CHAPTER FOUR

The ChiWalking Technique

When you have worn out your shoes, the strength of the shoe leather has passed into the fiber of your body . . . He is the richest man who pays the largest debt to his shoemaker.—RALPH WALDO EMERSON

I love watching sporting events, not because I really care who wins, but because I love to watch how people move and use their bodies. When I was a child, my mother told me, I would study (and study and study) kids riding their bikes before I would try. But then, she told me, I jumped on and rode off as if I'd been riding a bike for years. Since then I have applied the same approach to body movement. So I study the top athletes in order to understand how to move in the most efficient way.

Walking is such a basic human movement. We can't help but believe that we're doing it right. It's what we're meant to do. The stresses of life, however, have a cumulative effect on the amount of muscular tension we hold in our bodies. Most of us have taken on movement patterns that are constricted, at times to the point of being detrimental to our health.

The images of beauty that marketing companies constantly throw at us also influence our movement and posture. Browse through any fashion magazine and notice the models: their hips are thrust forward and often twisted in the most exaggerated ways. Unfortunately, most of us have taken on this stance to some extent. I would venture to guess that about 90 percent of all Americans over the age of 10 stand with their hips too far forward or out to one side. Just this one aspect of your posture can throw off the efficiency of your walking and affect every step you take—not to mention the health of your lower back.

The good news is we can learn to walk in the way we were meant to walk: tall, centered, strong, and energetic. If you need an example of good walking technique, just watch small children as they move about. Those little folks may not have much height, but they stand to their full stature and have the perfect gait. Study their movement and compare it to adults', and you'll see a world of difference. Dr. Ozzie Gontang, a psychologist with a focus on exercise and mental health, has been teaching this way of walking for more than thirty years to his thousands of patients in the San Diego area with profound results.

Here's what one of my clients said:

I can't believe the difference when I walk using your technique. I had back pain and soreness after long walks, and now I feel I could go forever. I thought walking would be the best way to recover from my surgery, but I found I'd gotten so out of shape, even walking seemed like an effort. Now I practice my posture all day long, and when I hit that hill outside my home, I take small steps and lean in a bit, and I get to the top with no trouble—thanks so much. You've made getting back into shape really enjoyable. —*Eric*

The key to making the most of your walking is to walk with correct technique, which you'll learn about in this chapter. You will first Body Sense how you currently walk and then you'll send your body this new information to try out. Becoming a better walker is not dependent on how fast or how far you can walk, but on how *well* you can listen to your body and how *well* you can respond to its needs.

In this chapter you will learn the fundamentals of good walking form. With a smooth and efficient walking technique, you'll have access to the many benefits offered by ChiWalking. In chapter 5 we'll present the ChiWalking Menu—twelve different walks, each a variation on this basic technique. Some walks will be slower and more relaxed, and some will be faster and more energetic and vibrant. But the basic ChiWalking technique will be the foundation underlying all of the various walks and supporting all of your movement in general.

The basic ChiWalking technique is broken down into "bite-sized" pieces for easy learning. These pieces are called Form Focuses and will become the "tools of your trade." Like a pianist learning a new piece of music, we'll break down the components of walking into smaller pieces and then work to slowly incorporate each of the new movements into our body memory. Inherent in this approach is the principle of Gradual Progress, a fundamental principle in ChiWalking that has been taken from T'ai Chi.

GRADUAL PROGRESS:
A PRINCIPLE OF T'AI CHI AND A LAW OF NATURE

Gradual Progress is a universal law that applies to all things and in every situation. It says that everything must follow a simple pattern of growth, starting small and gradually increasing in size until it becomes its mature size. A tree, for example, starts from a seed and gradually grows taller until it reaches its full size. When a traffic jam happens, it starts with a couple of cars, then grows larger as more cars come along, adding to the congestion. When Buddha began teaching the practice of compassion, he had only a few students. As his popularity grew, he took on more students until he had quite a following. Today there are millions of Buddhists all over the world.

There is nothing, from the atomic level on up, that does not follow this principle. It's called a universal law, because everyone and everything has to follow it in order to progress as they naturally should. Of course, we all have freedom of choice; that's the enigmatic human quality that holds us apart from everything else in creation, and that's where most of us screw up. When we do things out of order and try to get things done out of turn, we break this immutable law and end up suffering the consequences of our actions. If you're trying to bake a cake, you don't turn up the heat to *get it done* faster. It will burn. It needs warm heat over time to transform the ingredients into cake. If you want to marry someone, you don't start off by planning the wedding. It's always best if you begin by dating the person first, just to see if you like them. Then you look for compatibility and qualities that you admire. You slowly build a friendship that can then turn into a relationship. As you work on your communication skills and allow the partnership to grow in depth and mutual respect, at some point you might become aware that you *have* a marriage of two people, a partnership. And when you finally decide to let everyone else in on your secret, you might choose to celebrate with a wedding.

Any process happens best when it happens gradually over time. It's the law of Gradual Progress, and if you work within the law, you'll have the support of Nature backing up your actions. So when you're learning the ChiWalking form, follow the law and start slowly in small ways. Don't try to learn it all at once or perfect it overnight. It takes a lifetime to master something, so be easy on yourself and keep your expectations reasonable. Walking moves at the speed it does for one big reason: it doesn't *need* to go any faster than it does. If you want to go faster, you can always try ChiRunning.

The principle of Gradual Progress is woven throughout this book, and whenever it's mentioned, just pause and think about what it means to you. When you can recognize it easily, you'll be less likely to violate it, and your life will move forward without all the "bumps" you create by pushing the pace.

TIPS FOR EASIER LEARNING

Before we dive into the nuts and bolts of the ChiWalking technique, I'd like to offer a few tips to make your learning process easier and more fun.

START SIMPLE

Relax! Don't feel as though you have to learn all of the Form Focuses right away. Take it *slowly* and you'll learn more *quickly*. The best things in life take time to develop, so allow yourself the necessary time to learn the Form Focuses and to grow into your ChiWalking technique. Do only the amount that you can do well and don't sweat the rest—it'll come. Be sure to celebrate all of your small successes.

Practice the ChiWalking focuses that you feel will do you the most good up front, then let the others follow as you feel ready to take on more. For some people this might mean posture work, for others it might be first learning to relax. At some point you'll be surprised to find out that you can carry on five focuses at once because you will have incorporated into your body what you practiced.

When you've mastered the ChiWalking focuses, you'll have a number of tools that you'll be able to use simultaneously, which you can apply to your walking as well as to your life. For those of you with a penchant for multitasking, this is a dream come true.

KNOW WHICH FOCUS
YOU'LL BE WORKING ON

Before heading out for your walk, familiarize yourself with the specific Form Focus or Focuses that you'll be practicing. If necessary, refer back to this book and reread the description of the focus so that you know exactly what to do.

The more thorough you are in knowing and understanding each of the ChiWalking focuses, the sooner you'll be gliding down the road with impeccable form. What you'll be doing for yourself in the long term is reprogramming your brain and body to move in a healthier and more efficient way.

Learn the ChiWalking focuses correctly up front so that improper movement habits don't become problems later on. In chapter 3 I mentioned qualitative exactitude and in this chapter you'll get to practice it. When you take the time to perfect your use of the ChiWalking focuses they will be an invaluable asset later on when you apply them. For instance, if you learn good postural alignment and breathing now, you'll have two valuable energy-producing tools to use for the rest of your life.

BE CONSISTENT IN YOUR EFFORTS

Learning new movement habits takes persistence and consistency. Whenever you're learning something new in your body, the best way to retain that knowledge is to repeat the motion or exercise as often as possible. Your body and your mind both learn best by repetition, so the more you practice each Form Focus, the sooner you'll be able to build muscle memory and eventually master each movement.

At first you might run into some awkwardness or discomfort with doing something that's different from what you're used to. Your body might even offer some resistance to the improvement. That's totally natural. How many times were you told as a child to eat your vegetables because your mother said they were good for you? Well, they *were* good for you, and after eating them as an adult you can now see the value of eating good food.

Most of the ChiWalking Form Focuses can be practiced whether you're walking or not. You can be practicing your posture while you're driving your car or working on your breathing while watching a movie. Don't limit yourself as to when you practice your ChiWalking focuses. Get creative and practice your focuses regularly so that they become second nature to you. Look for ways you can use them throughout your day, and you'll have the beginnings of living a mindful life.

When you begin walking, commit to exercising four days a week or every other day at least. When you're learning something new, it helps to have your practice sessions somewhat close together so that you're not starting from scratch with the learning process each time you go out.

HAVE GOALS, BUT RELISH THE PROCESS

Whether you want to use your walking to lose weight, get physically fit, or train for a specific event, set clear goals for yourself *but* put your attention into the *process* and you'll enjoy each workout much more. Focus on your surroundings, on feeling your body move freely through space, on the feeling of success when you master a new skill. You're way more likely to arrive at your goal when you enjoy each step along the way.

PRACTICE 1-MINUTE FORM INTERVALS AS A LEARNING TOOL

A very effective way to learn the Form Focuses is to use a countdown timer, available on many sports watches. (For ChiWalking, a sports watch with a countdown timer is one of the most important pieces of equipment, besides good walking shoes.) Let's say you're working on leveling your pelvis. Before beginning your walk, stand still and practice leveling your pelvis a few times. Then, before you begin your walk, set your timer to beep at 1-minute intervals. As you begin your walk, start your timer and practice holding your pelvis level for 1 minute. Don't have your mind on anything but leveling your pelvis. When your beeper goes off, spend a minute just relaxing your mind and don't focus on anything particular. When your beeper goes off again, be mindful of leveling your pelvis again for a solid minute. Repeat this on-and-off mode for the duration of your walk.

By focusing for a minute and then not focusing for a minute, your body will quickly learn how to reengage each focus in an instant. If you're out for a 30-minute walk, you'll be engaging and focusing your mind fifteen times, which is probably many more times than if you were to go out for a walk without a plan.

WALK WITH A FRIEND

Because it can be somewhat difficult to tell whether or not you're doing a focus correctly, get a friend to learn ChiWalking too, so that you can help each other remember the focuses. Check in with each other to see if you understand what each focus is and how it's done. Offer each other help and suggestions with your individual techniques. If you walk regularly with a friend or a group of friends, mutually agree to work on your focuses for at least the first 15 minutes of every walk. Once your focuses are engaged, you'll all have an easier time remembering to do them while talking and enjoying each other's company.

A second, wonderful benefit of walking with a friend is that you can help each other stay consistent with your ChiWalking programs. It's so much easier to get out of the door and walk when you know that a friend is waiting for you.

TRAINING TOOLS AND EQUIPMENT

THE METRONOME

As you can see from the walking Menu, all of the specific walks have a suggested cadence range given in *strides per minute* (spm). The best piece of equipment I've ever found for this is a small electronic metronome that clips onto the waistband of your pants. (These nifty little metronomes are available on our Web site: www.ChiWalking.com.) It emits a steady beat that you can match your stride to. The speed of the metronome can be manually set faster or slower depending on what cadence you're walking at.

How to Use the Metronome

Go to the ChiWalking Matrix on page 137 and choose the walk you'd like to do. Then look up the cadence range at the bottom of the page. Before you begin walking, *set* the metronome to the lower number in the cadence range and turn the beeper off. Then, once you're warmed up, turn on your metronome and match your walking stride rate to the beep from the metronome. Remember, the cadence numbers in the ChiWalking Matrix are for the stride rate of only one of your legs. Pick your favorite leg and match its stride rate to the metronome.

If your cadence feels too slow for the type of walk you're doing, bump up the speed of the metronome one beep at a time until your stride rate feels right.

THE HEART RATE MONITOR

For those of you wanting to know exactly what your heart is doing at any time during your walking, I suggest getting a heart rate monitor. There are many types available, from a simple model that measures your heart rate to the high-end model that plugs into a computer and records everything from your heart rate at various points along your walk to your speed and distance. Prices range from $40 to $400. Simpler is better, but get one that allows you to input the upper limit of your heart rate. This is a good safety and informational tool to let you know when you've reached your heart rate limit relative to the type of walk you're doing.

How to Use the Heart Rate Monitor

Go to the ChiWalking Matrix and look up the suggested heart rate range at the bottom of the page (% MHR). Since the numbers listed are written as a percentage of your maximum heart rate, you'll have to first calculate your maximum heart rate. The easiest way to do this is to subtract your age in years from the number 220. This method is a generally accepted number to go by. If you are under the care of a doctor, you can ask what your maximum heart rate should be.

Watch the readout on your wrist monitor and keep your heart rate close to your projected number. If your heart rate is too slow, pick up your cadence until your heart rate settles at the number you're shooting for. Conversely, slow your cadence down if your heart rate is too fast. (More information in Chapter 5.)

Another use of the heart rate monitor is to teach yourself to be a more efficient walker. Choose a walk that's designed to elevate your heart rate. When you're well into the walk, check your heart rate, then try to see if you can lower your heart rate while maintaining the same walking speed. This can be done by working with various ChiWalking Form Focuses, such as relaxing your muscles, breathing fully, engaging your core, or rotating your pelvis.

THE PEDOMETER

According to the AARP (American Association of Retired Persons) and the American Council on Fitness and Nutrition, taking 10,000 steps a day will not only keep you fit, but if your daily caloric intake remains constant, you can lose up to a pound a week.

The average adult takes between 2,000 and 4,000 steps per day, which translates to 1 to 2 miles. Using a pedometer is also a great way to make your walking program more fun. Most people think they walk farther each day than they do, and the pedometer is a fun way to find out how much you actually walk.

How to Use the Pedometer

At the beginning of your day, set your pedometer to 0 and clip it to your waistband, then read it again at the end of your day, when you're putting on your pajamas. Note the number in your journal for future reference.

Measure the number of steps you take each day for three days in a row to get an idea of your daily average. If this number is less than 10,000 steps per day, try to increase your number of daily steps by *no more than* 20 percent each week until you reach that magic number. If your goal is to go beyond 10,000 steps per day, just follow this same progression. Remember, your daily steps don't have to be done all at once. They can be spread out over the entire day.

Here are some suggestions to help increase your number of daily steps:

- take the stairs instead of the elevator
- walk during your lunch hour
- park your car a block or two away from your destination

or, make up your own creative ways to take more steps.

SHOES

For Walking

Unless you walk barefoot, your shoes are all that separates you from the surface you're walking on. So it's important to wear a shoe that meets your needs and matches your abilities. Having a good pair of walking shoes can certainly make a difference in your walking experience. A shoe designed to move well with your body will give you many more miles of pleasure. The basic guidelines for shoes are simple:

- Fit is important. They should not feel too big or too small. Allow plenty of room in the "toe box" to allow your toes good circulation.
- Your shoes should feel so comfortable that you could use them for bedroom slippers.

- Summer walking shoes should be breathable so that your feet don't sweat.
- Shoes should be very flexible in the forefoot, not stiff.
- The heels should be low to the ground, not built up like running shoes.

Shall We Walk?

Okay, it's time to get your shoes on because here's where the rubber meets the road. We will now take you through all of the Form Focuses in the ChiWalking technique. In no time, you'll be able to sense the difference it makes in your walking.

Let's begin with an overview of what you'll be aiming for in terms of the ChiWalking technique, so that you'll have a sense of the new movement habits you'll be taking on.

THE OVERVIEW

Simply put, the art of ChiWalking involves learning to have a slight lean when you walk. In this way, you'll be taking advantage of the pull of gravity because, as you lean, gravity pulls you forward, providing most of your forward propulsion. This huge force is at our disposal *all* the time.

T'ai Chi is a martial art that teaches the practitioner how to move *with* the forces of Nature as well as the force of an opponent. You don't meet an opponent's punch with a punch. You move with the force of his punch, thereby neutralizing its impact. When you walk correctly, you are allowing your body to move forward with a controlled fall, working with gravity rather than against it.

Moving *with* the pull of gravity requires that you keep your body aligned but *relaxed*. In this way gravity can pull your body forward without meeting with any stiffness, which inhibits easy flow. Your legs mainly serve to support your body weight between strides.

The ChiWalking technique will ask you to

- concentrate on maintaining good posture whenever you're walking or standing;

- pick up your feet when you walk;
- walk with a shorter stride than you're used to;
- allow your spine to twist and your pelvis to rotate;
- extend your stride behind you instead of reaching forward with your stride (this rearward stride will come from the rotation of your pelvis);
- relax your arms and legs so they'll swing more easily (when your limbs are relaxed they offer little or no resistance to your forward motion);
- lean slightly forward when you walk, landing with your feet directly underneath your center of gravity as you move forward.

Figure 8—Plant your foot underneath your center of gravity as you step forward

LEARNING THE CHIWALKING TECHNIQUE USING THE FIVE MINDFUL STEPS

This five-step method is a useful tool to take you from start to finish in almost any circumstance, so we'll use it here as a tool for learning the ChiWalking technique. Here's how it applies. The first three steps of the Five Mindful Steps are used to adjust your posture. The fourth and fifth steps come into play when you actually begin walking.

1. You'll **get aligned** by lining up your shoulders, hip bones, and ankles into a vertical line.
2. You'll learn how to **engage your core** by leveling your pelvis and leading with your upper body.
3. We'll explain how to **create balance** throughout your body while you're walking.

4. You'll **make a choice** as to which focuses you will mindfully practice.
5. Here we'll have you **move forward** into a healthier way of walking by practicing your ChiWalking focuses every step of the way.

With all of that said and done, let's get rolling!

ALIGN YOURSELF AND ENGAGE YOUR CORE: CREATE YOUR BEST POSTURE

I start every student off, regardless of her previous experience, with learning how to maintain good posture while walking. The quality of your posture has a direct influence on the quality of

your walking. With good posture supporting your body, your walking will be graceful and efficient. You'll quickly see that by keeping your posture aligned, using your core muscles, and walking in balance, you'll finish every walk feeling rejuvenated from head to toe.

Chi moves more easily through a body that is both aligned and relaxed.

In the following exercises we'll refer to your posture as your *column*. Your column is the central axis running vertically through your body and it supports your body weight while standing or walking. Having good posture allows your body to be supported by your bones, ligaments, and tendons, not by your muscles. When I see someone who has stood with poor posture for most of her life, I see someone with tight neck muscles (from holding her head up),

Figure 9—Posture stance showing the alignment of the column

tight lower back muscles (from having underdeveloped abdominals), and overdeveloped calf muscles (from having to support an unbal-

Figure 10—"Connecting the dots"

anced upper body). When I see someone with nice straight posture, I usually see someone with relaxed muscles from head to toe, because his posture is in balance and his structure is supporting his body weight. I can't say enough about how much healthier your body (and your outlook) is when you have good posture.

Here are the four steps to creating great posture. What you're aiming for is to have a straight line running through your shoulders, hip bones, and ankles. I call it "connecting the dots."

Step 1. Align Your Feet

Start by aligning your feet. Look down and make sure your feet are hip width apart and parallel. Soften your knees so that they're not locked. (Injury prevention tip: If your feet turn out when you stand, as many people's do, your medial meniscus tendon will be pulled with each step, eventually causing knee pain. To alleviate this, simply rotate your *entire* leg in toward your centerline until your foot is pointing forward. (If this feels like a strain, rotate your leg in only as far as feels comfortable, then gradually rotate your leg inward in small increments and increase the amount of rotation slightly, week by week.) Aligning your feet will help to relax tight piriformis muscles (which lie beneath the gluteus maximus). Don't worry; you're not alone. Most of us hold tension in our pelvic area. We're all tight-asses.

Step 2. Align Your Upper Body

Next, align your upper body by putting one hand on your belly button and the other hand just under your collarbone. Lift up with your upper hand while pulling down with your lower hand. This straightens your upper spine and opens up your chest so that you can breathe easier. (For a complete explanation, refer to chapter 3 for "Breathing.") Rest your chin on your forefinger. This aligns your neck with the rest of your posture and helps eliminate neck pain while walking or standing.

Figure 11—Straightening the upper body

Figure 12—Proper head position

Step 3. Level Your Pelvis

Level your pelvis using your lower abdominals. This engages your core muscles and helps you to hold your posture straight while walking or standing.

To level your pelvis, lift up slightly on your pubic bone using your *lower* abdominal muscles. The lowest of these muscles is called the

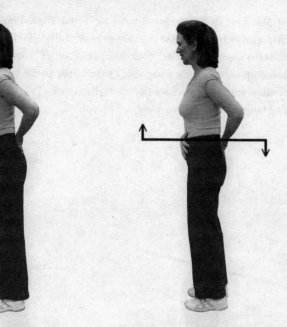

Figure 13a—Pelvis not level (notice waistband is tilted forward)

Figure 13b—Pelvis level (notice waistband is level)

pyramidalis, which attaches to the pubic bone. Be sure you're not using your glutes to level your pelvis, as this will restrict your leg swing and keep you from strengthening your abs. You need to Body Sense how to level your pelvis correctly. I call it "the vertical crunch" because that's what it feels like you're doing. (If you can't feel your lower abdominal muscles, just place your hand below your belly button and cough, and you'll feel them engage.)

Master Xu, my T'ai Chi teacher, says that your pelvis is like a bowl holding water. When it tilts down in front, all of your water (your chi) will spill out. So keep it level and you'll gather energy to your center (*dantien*).

If you have too much curvature in your lower spine, you could be in for increasing bouts with lower back pain. Leveling the pelvis is one of the best exercises for anyone suffering from lower back pain. Strong abdominals allow your lower back to flatten out, which in turn relieves compression on your lumbar discs. If your pelvis doesn't come up to level right away, don't worry. Just do the best you can, but remind yourself to constantly strengthen those lower abdominals all day long. Your lower back will thank you.

Figure 14a—Too much curvature in the lower spine

Figure 14b—Right amount of curvature in the lower spine

A good way to remember to hold your posture straight and your pelvis level is to imagine your body making the shape of the letter *C*. Your spine is straight, your chin is down, and your pelvis is coming up in front. *C* is for Core strength, Centeredness, and having a Container for your Chi, all of which come from leveling your pelvis. If you don't level your pelvis, your *C* is reversed and you spill your chi.

Figure 15a—Correct posture showing the C-shape

Figure 15b—Incorrect posture

Step 4. Tilt Your Statue

Once you've leveled your pelvis, the next step is to *tilt your statue*. Imagine that your upper body, from the point where your legs meet your pelvis, to the top of your head, is one solid unit, like the bust of a statue. Then, *tilt your statue* ¼ inch forward. When you first tilt your upper body in this way, you might feel like you're tipping forward. You're not. If you normally stand with your shoulders behind your hips, as most people do, you'll be tipping yourself more toward a straight vertical line and into *true balance*. I say "true balance" because your centerline will be directly over your feet. If you're doing it correctly, you should feel your abdominal muscles engage. That's because you're now using your abdominals to help hold your posture, where you weren't doing so before. Practice this regularly, and you

will have a strong set of abs, a healthy lower back, and your posture
will be in perfect balance—directly over your feet.

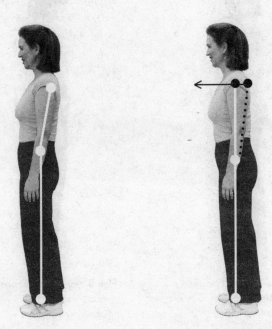

Figure 16a—Tilt the statue (before)   **Figure 16b—Tilt the statue (after)**

Another way to feel and maintain the straightness of your posture
is to push up with the crown of your head, like you're trying to "hold
up the sky."

Never lock your knees when you're standing. It will block the chi
flow through your legs and ruin your knees. They should always be
slightly bent, and your weight should be evenly distributed between
your heels and the balls of your feet.

After completing these steps, you will have great posture, which I
refer to as your *column*.

These principles of alignment are no different than the postural
alignment taught in any Feldenkrais, Alexander Technique, Pilates,
yoga, T'ai Chi, or dance class. It might feel like a lot of work to hold

Figure 17—Side view of the column

your body in this position, but you will eventually sense the straightness of your posture. And when you do, there is nothing like it. You'll feel like a pipe that has just been straightened out, and the water that has been backed up can begin to flow again.

MEMORIZE WHAT GOOD POSTURE FEELS LIKE

Once you've done the four steps to align your posture, just stand still and memorize what it feels like to stand straight and tall. It might feel foreign or familiar, but whatever it is, memorize the body sensation that you're feeling by taking a "snapshot" with your mind's eye. Return to this position over and over again—many times each day until you can Body Sense correct posture stance whenever you're standing and *especially* when you're over your weight-bearing leg while walking. A trick that I use to remember to watch my posture is to set my watch to beep once an hour. When it goes off I do a quick posture adjustment and continue on with my day. If you don't have an alarm of some kind, you can use main transitions in your day to remind yourself to check in with your posture: for example, getting into and out of the car, standing up from your desk, walking to and from your office.

PRACTICE GOOD POSTURE ALL THE TIME

Practice getting yourself aligned with your posture *all the time*. When you're waiting for a bus, or standing in line at the bank, or talking to a friend, focus on posture. The better you get at engaging your posture at odd times, the easier it will be to remember to do it while you're walking.

My T'ai Chi teacher used to have me practice my posture stance in class for 90 minutes twice a week. He'd tell me to just stand there, without moving. He would then walk away and teach his other students for 20 minutes before returning, only to make some small adjustment in my posture and leave me standing there for another 20 minutes. This went on for the first month of class. Although it was somewhat annoying at the time, I now appreciate the importance of what he was trying to teach me. When I can sense my posture slipping out of alignment I can quickly and easily make slight adjustments to straighten myself up in the moment.

CHECK YOUR POSTURE FOR CORRECTNESS

It's good to check in with an outside source to see if your posture is actually straight. Here's the easiest way I've found to check for good posture. After you've straightened yourself and "connected your dots," look down to see if you can see your shoelaces. If your hips are too far forward, as most people's are, you won't be able to see them. But if you're aligned properly, they'll be there. You can also ask a friend to look at you from the side and tell you if your shoulders, hips, and ankles are in a straight line. If they're not, ask your friend to manually adjust your body until your dots are connected. Standing sideways to a full-length mirror also works.

Here's a great exercise to get you to feel the huge difference between good posture and poor posture. It will also give you a very clear sense of engaging your core muscles.

Figure 18—Looking down to see your shoelaces

The Pull-down Exercise

Do this with a friend. Stand with your entire body relaxed as if you had never heard of working on your posture. Then, have your friend stand behind you and gently pull down on your shoulders. If you're like most people, your back will bend backward and your belly will move forward, showing you that your column is not strong.

Figure 19a—Stand with your core relaxed

Figure 19b—Pull down gently on the shoulders (notice the hips move forward)

Figure 19c—Pull down with your core engaged

Now, stand upright again and do this. Engage your posture using the four steps previously mentioned:

1. Align your feet
2. Straighten your upper spine
3. Level your pelvis
4. Tilt your statue 1/4 inch forward

When you have aligned your posture, have your friend pull down on your shoulders again—and feel the difference. You should feel strong and solid as a tree trunk. This little demonstration will give you an unmistakable sense of having your posture aligned and your core engaged.

After you've practiced your posture stance to the point of familiarity, the next thing you'll be working on will be adding motion to your alignment.

MAKE A CHOICE: LEAD WITH YOUR UPPER BODY AND YOUR FEET WILL FOLLOW

Your legs are like a movable support system. Each time your foot comes down on the ground, your leg momentarily supports your body weight. Your legs make it possible for you to walk, but they should not be the source of your movement. The real source of your walking is the pull of gravity.

Your choice is this: You can either walk (as most people do) by leading with your hips and legs, which forces your *legs* to do all of the work of propelling your body forward. Or you can lead with your upper body, letting gravity pull you along as your upper body falls gently forward. Then, your legs will swing to the rear with each stride.

When most people walk, they swing their legs *forward* with each stride, leading with their hips. As they do this, they lock their knees and strike the ground with their heels. This causes impact to their knees because, as their heel strikes in front of their body, they're momentarily stopping their forward momentum with every stride. Moving in this way also makes your body go up and down, which is an inefficient way to walk, especially over long distances.

With the ChiWalking technique you will be straightening your knees as you *finish* your stride behind your body, and your foot will return to its beginning position underneath your center of gravity, not out in front of you. This takes all the impact off of your knees, and you'll reduce the work your quads have to do.

Try this exercise to Body Sense what I'm talking about. You can even do it while you're reading this book.

- First, stand up tall with your best posture. Don't lock your knees, but soften them a little.
- Now shift your weight to one of your legs and let that leg support your entire body weight. We call this a one-legged posture stance.

Now you have a choice. You can either extend your free leg out in front of your body, locking your knee and letting your heel rest on the ground (this is the position that most walkers are in when they initi-

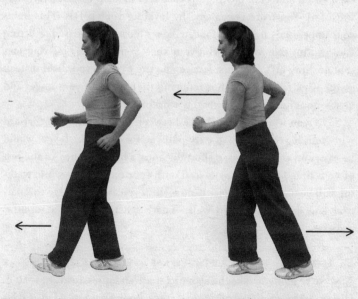

Figure 20a—Leg swinging forward incorrectly

Figure 20b—Correct leg extension to the rear (notice how the rear leg straightens)

ate a step forward), or you can shift your weight onto one leg and extend your free leg out behind your body, resting your foot on the
ground with your knee straightened. This is the position your body
will be in when you're ChiWalking. Your weight will be over your
lead leg while your opposite leg is extended out the back.

Here's the difference between the two. In figure 20a, your forward
leg *pulls* you forward during the first phase of your stride, and then
pushes you forward once your body passes over your foot. This does a
number of things: your hamstrings are overworked because they are
pulling you forward, your knees are taking some shock with each heel
strike, and, odds are, you are compressing your lower back. As you
push off with your toes, you run the risk of overusing your calves and
shins, which are susceptible to injury.

In figure 20b your body is being propelled forward by the pull of
gravity while your trailing leg extends behind you. The only *work* required by your legs is straightening your knees at the back end of
each stride and then picking up your feet to keep up with your forward fall. Your core is engaged by leveling your pelvis. This holds
your upper body over your foot strike with each stride. You're lifting
your trailing foot forward with your knee, gently rolling off your toes
(not pushing off), and then landing on the *front* of your heel instead
of the back of the heel, thus reducing the impact to your knees and
quads. Your hamstrings are barely working, if at all.

So, if you were given a choice between pulling yourself forward
with your legs or having gravity pull you forward, which way would
be easier on your body for a short distance, a long distance, or the rest
of your life? The only way to lead with your upper body while walking will be to *make the choice* to do so until you are rewired to this natural and efficient way to walk. That's what makes it a mindful
exercise.

MOVING FORWARD: LOWER-BODY FOCUSES

Now we're going to take the above exercise and move forward with it.
Here's a slow-motion drill to give you a Body Sense of what it feels
like to lead with your upper body and land with your foot underneath you.

In the practice of T'ai Chi, you are taught to move very slowly through a routine of consecutive movements. This slow motion allows you to move through all of the various positions while practicing balance, relaxation, strength, and looseness in each. If you move too quickly at first, your body will have a more difficult time discerning what is right and wrong about your movement. For this reason, I suggest you do this exercise slowly so that you can feel the correct alignment and movement of your body.

- Begin by standing in your best posture stance with your knees slightly bent.
- Shift your weight to your left leg and feel for your one-legged posture stance.
- Take your right leg and extend it a short distance behind you. You should be able to easily rest your heel on the ground with your knee bent. This will give you a good feeling of what your optimal stride length should be.
- Now, straighten your right leg and shift all of your weight onto your left leg by bringing your upper body directly over your left foot. At the same time you'll be gently rolling your right foot off the ground and swinging your leg forward with your knee. The only time your knee is straightened is at the back of your stride, just before you lift your knee forward to take a step. As you straighten your knee, you should feel your pelvis rotate in the direction of your straightened leg.

The natural movement of your pelvis is to always rotate toward your straightening leg. As your pelvis rotates in this way, you'll be able to feel the twist in your spine.

PICK UP YOUR HEELS AND
RELAX YOUR LOWER LEGS

Here you'll learn to relax your lower legs so that you do not overwork them by pushing off with your toes. In ChiWalking, since gravity does the bulk of the work of moving you forward, your lower legs can truly relax and take a backseat.

The Standing Heel Lift

- First I want you to feel the difference between picking up your heels and pushing off with your toes. Start by pushing your foot up off the ground with your toes. You should be able to feel all the muscles in your toes, ankles, and calves working to push your foot up.

- Now, with your ankle and lower leg relaxed, lift your heel up off the ground and imagine that you're peeling your foot off the ground as if it were a postage stamp you're peeling off a roll. You shouldn't feel any pressure under your toes or feet as you lift. Your ankle should be so relaxed that your toes drop down as you pick up your heel. Can you feel the difference?

The Walking Heel Lift

- Get into your best posture and begin walking while lifting your heel up over your opposite ankle. Walk this way for 20 steps. Relax your ankles and let your toes drop down each time you lift your heels. Your ankles should be so relaxed that your toes drop down each time you pick up one of your heels.

- Now switch to walking as you normally do. You should feel the balls of your feet and your toes pressing against the ground. You'll feel every muscle, ligament, and tendon in your lower legs tense up. That's a waste of energy! Walking by pushing yourself off with your toes will either set you up for injury or leave you with over-developed shin and calf muscles. That's because your lower leg muscles are not meant to propel you forward.

- Now switch back to picking up your heels and feel how the ball of your foot is not pressing against the ground as much with every step. Walk this way until you can keep your lower legs relaxed with every step you take. Feel how good your lower legs feel when they're relaxed.

Pelvic Rotation

Chubby Checker was right, we all need to be doing "the Twist."

The rotation of your pelvis and the twist of your spine are two of the keys to good walking form. Yes, everything else is important too. But your ability to move your hips and pelvis is what will make great walking possible. And having good movement in your pelvis is directly dependent on your ability to let your spine twist.

Do the Twist

Here's an exercise that will help you to learn to rotate your pelvis and feel the twist along your spine.

- Begin by standing with your feet hip width apart in your best posture stance. Have your knees slightly bent with your weight evenly distributed between your legs. Be sure that you're leveling your pelvis during this exercise.

Figure 21—Your pelvis rotates as your hip goes back with the rear leg

- Shift your weight onto one of your legs so that you're standing in a one-legged posture stance.
- Keeping your weight directly over your support leg, take your free leg and extend it behind your body with your heel comfortably on the ground. (Note: Your hip goes back

Figure 22a—Beginning position: Hold your arms as if you're in an armchair

with your rear leg and your spine twists with it. Your weight should be 60 percent on your forward leg and 40 percent on your back leg.

- Hold your arms at your sides with your elbows bent at a 90-degree angle and your palms down. Pretend you're resting your elbows on the arms of an armchair.

- Imagine that there is an axis that runs vertically through your body. It's a centerline around which your body rotates. Once you can Body Sense your centerline, hold your arms in a stable position and

Figure 22b—Rotate your pelvis to the left

rotate your pelvis back and forth around your centerline.

- Start by rotating your pelvis slowly and pick up the speed as your movement begins to feel more familiar. As you get even more used to rotating your pelvis, you can increase the amount of your pelvic rotation.

This is a fun exercise for loosening your pelvis. You'll be at the head of the class when you take up salsa dancing. It will leave

Figure 22c—Rotate your pelvis to the right

you with a distinct feeling of being able to rotate your pelvis while holding it level at the same time. You cannot practice this too much, so do it as often as you can. I like to use it as a lower-back-loosening exercise whenever I've been desk-bound for too long.

THE IMPORTANCE OF CADENCE AND STRIDE LENGTH

Your stride should be a comfortable length, and you should feel no burning sensation on the back of your heel, which would mean you're overstretching your Achilles tendon. Once you have established a comfortable stride length for yourself, it is important to keep it a consistent length *no matter what speed you're walking*. The only thing that changes with your stride is your cadence, the rate at which your feet hit the ground. As you walk faster, your cadence will increase, but not your stride length. If you watch racewalkers, you'll notice that their stride is not very long even though they might be walking at an 8-minute-per-mile pace. It's their cadence that is turning over at a rapid rate. So the principle is this: if you want to walk faster, simply increase your cadence but always keep your stride length the same. To increase your cadence, simply bend your arms more and swing them faster.

Stride length and cadence are some of the major differences between ChiWalking and ChiRunning. For those of you who have practiced ChiRunning, you will note that it is just the opposite with running. Your cadence always stays the same and your stride length changes as you increase or decrease your speed.

Figure 23—Your stride should remain at a comfortable length

First practice walking at 60 strides per minute (spm), then at 65 spm, then at 70 spm, and finally at 75 spm. Each of these cadences needs to be done for only a brief period of time. Just enough to give you a body sense of how your cadence—*not* your stride length— changes as you go faster. Keeping your statue tilted ¼ inch will ensure that your upper body always remains slightly ahead of your support leg. Your lower leg should remain passive at all times and your ankles should always be loose and relaxed.

The best way to *move forward* is to get your entire body to move as a single fluid unit. This begins with balancing the movement of your upper body with that of your lower body so that neither part is doing more than its fair share of the work. If you're used to powering your walking solely with your legs, you'll be rewiring your nervous system to rely less on your legs and to allow your upper body to help out more. Conversely, if your upper body is not relaxed and moving freely, your legs will have to carry a far greater share of the workload.

UPPER-BODY FOCUSES

Although conventional wisdom would lead you to believe that your upper body includes everything above your waist, I define "upper body" as everything above the point on your spine where the curve in your upper back meets the curve in your lower back. That's because in the ChiWalking technique, every-thing above this point moves with the upper body and everything be-low this point moves with the lower body. As these two sections of your body rotate opposite to each other, a natural twist occurs along the spine. The center of this twist is at T-12/L-1, which is the medical term for

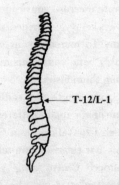

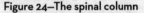 ← T-12/L-1

Figure 24—The spinal column

where your twelfth (lowest) thoracic vertebra meets your first lumbar vertebra (see figure 24). In traditional Chinese medicine this is one of the main points where chi enters the body. This is an important spot

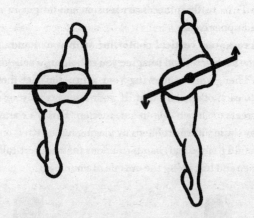

Figure 25—Pelvis not rotating and pelvis rotating

to be aware of, because when your spine twists at this point, more chi energy will enter your body, thus energizing you while you walk. It's as close as Nature has ever come to creating a perpetual motion machine, because the more you use it, the more energy it generates.

Here are some upper-body focuses that will help to balance out the work of your lower body.

- **Bend your elbows** (See figure 26A). The amount of bend in your arms will depend on how fast you'd like to walk. For a medium-paced walk, bend your arms at the same angle you would have them at if you were just putting your hands in your pants pockets—just below your waist. The less you bend at the elbows, the slower you'll walk. As you walk faster, you'll need to bend your elbows more and swing your arms more vigorously. During your slowest walks, your arms will swing fully extended at your sides. When you're doing a fast walk, your arms will remain bent at 90 degrees at all times, which means that your hands will never fall below your waistband. This will make them swing faster and subsequently increase your cadence and your speed. Be careful to not hold your shoulders higher just because your hands are held higher. This creates unnecessary tension and fatigue in your shoulders and upper back.

- **Don't cross your vertical centerline with your hands.** Bend your elbows to 90 degrees and imagine you're holding a volleyball in your hands. Then, when you swing your arms, don't let them get any closer to each other than that. If your hands cross your centerline, you'll create too much side-to-side motion. This is a waste of energy and may cause future problems by placing undue stress on your hips, knees, and IT (iliotibial) bands (tendons that run vertically between your knee and hip, along the outside of your legs).

Figure 26a—Correct arm swing: your hands should never cross your centerline

Figure 26b—Incorrect arm swing: arms crossing the centerline

- **Relax your hands and wrists.** Walk with your fingers slightly curled in and your thumbs on top, as if you just caught a butterfly and you don't want to crush it. Hold your wrists straight but relaxed. Don't bend them back or hold any tension in them while walking. If you sense that you're holding tension during a walk, simply shake out your wrists every 5 or 10 minutes.

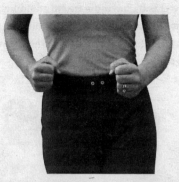

Figure 27a—Correct hand position: fingers lightly curled in

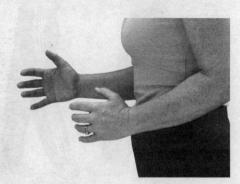

Figure 27b—Incorrect hand position: fingers extended

- **Keep your shoulders low and relaxed.** Your arms should hang down from your shoulders and not be held out away from the sides of your body when they swing. Too many people create neck and shoulder pain from holding their elbows out, away from their sides. If you tend to hold tension in your shoulders or upper back, let your arms totally dangle at your sides every 10 minutes during *every* walk. This way you can train yourself to constantly let go of any tension that you feel creeping in as you walk.

- **Swing your arms to the rear.** In ChiWalking, it is important to
  swing your arms to the rear, which creates a counterbalance to the
  forward lean of your column and the counterrotation of your
  pelvis. Practice this by having a friend stand behind you with her
  hands held about 6 inches behind your elbows. Swing your arms
  and try to hit her hands with your elbows. This will give you a
  sense of swinging your arms to the rear.

Figure 28—Practice swinging your elbows to the
rear with a friend

- **Keep your neck relaxed and aligned with your spine.** Don't
  stick your chin out or tilt your head back when you walk. Tuck your
  chin and reach for the sky with the crown of your head. This will
  straighten your neck and create more spaciousness in your upper
  spine. Keep your neck straight but relaxed. Look around while you

walk and don't hold your head straight forward all the time or you'll miss a lot of life.

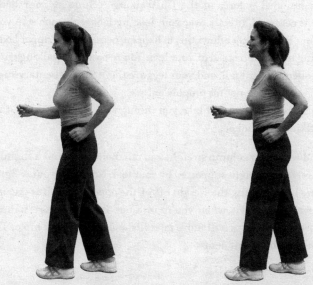

Figure 29a—Correct head position: eyes level and chin tucked

Figure 29b—Incorrect head position: don't stick your chin out

- **Relax your face, especially your jaw.** There is a huge tendency for many walkers to hold tension in their faces while walking. Watch out for clenching your teeth or squinting your eyes, especially as your walking speed increases.
- **Above all, level your pelvis and tilt your statue ¼ inch as you walk!** The two focuses most responsible for engaging the pull of gravity while you walk are leveling your pelvis and tilting your statue. Both work to keep your upper body aligned and forward as you walk.

It's important to have each of these focuses in place if you want your walking to be both energizing and relaxing. It's a lot to think about while you're walking, so when you're first learning the Chi-Walking technique, practice each of these upper-body focuses one at a time until you become familiar enough with all of them that you can keep them all going at once.

Taking Your First ChiWalking Steps

As I mentioned before, in the ChiWalking technique, your body weight is centered directly over your leading foot with each step you take. Your lean is what allows this to happen, because your upper body is leading the show instead of your legs. You're basically walking with a controlled forward fall, and your legs are there for momentary support of your body—not for propulsion.

The following steps will take you through all of the basics of the ChiWalking technique.

• Stand with your column straight and tall. Bend your knees slightly and feel your weight supported by your feet. Now shift your weight to one leg by taking the weight off of the opposite leg. It is crucial to level your pelvis when you're in a one-legged posture stance, otherwise your hips will move laterally and cause either hip or IT (iliotibial) band problems.

Figure 30a—When your core is disengaged, your hip goes lateral

Figure 30b—When your core is engaged, your alignment remains straight

- Stand in a one-legged posture stance for a few seconds, feeling your column supported by your foot. With all of your weight on your support leg, extend your unsupported leg behind you at a comfortable distance, resting your entire foot on the ground. This is your stride length and the position you should find yourself in at the end of each stride. Now, slowly swing your rear leg forward, landing on the front of your heel, then roll forward until you've established a new column of support directly over your newly placed foot. This exercise should be done very slowly so that you can feel your center move forward as your foot returns to its beginning position, underneath your body.

Figure 31a—Leg extends to the rear

Figure 31b—Weight on the support leg

(Note: It is important to keep your stride length comfortable and easily within your reach. This will keep you from overworking your legs and reduce your odds of developing a walking-related injury.)

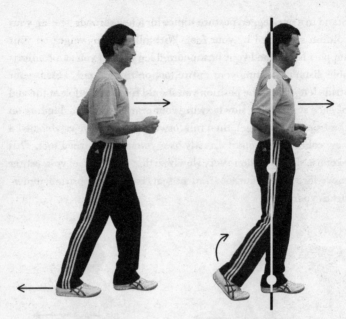

Figure 31c—Leg extends to the rear

Figure 31d—Weight on the support leg

- Now slowly shift your weight from one leg to the other while letting your column fall forward. In this way your upper body will be moving forward along with your knees and your body will move gracefully along the ground. Leaning forward allows your upper body to always stay directly over your support leg as your foot comes down onto the ground. Thus, with each step your center will be momentarily supported by your column as it falls forward. It is also important to keep your knee slightly bent as you swing your leg forward. (A common mistake made by many recreational walkers is to throw the leg forward, locking the knee as the foot hits the ground, which is hard on your knees.) Then, as you pass over your support foot, straighten your leg as it swings to the rear. The only part of your body that will move up and down will be your feet. Your knees will swing horizontally like two pendulums,

Figure 32—Align your column with each step you take

while your feet will describe an oval path. Practice walking slowly in this way until you can get a sense of what it feels like to walk with the pull of gravity while picking up your feet to keep up with your forward fall.

- With each stride, allow your spine to twist and your pelvis to rotate. You can feel this happening by locating T-12/L-1 and allowing your entire lower body below this point to rotate with each stride. When you allow your pelvis to rotate, you'll feel your hips alternately pulled to the rear by your trailing leg. Many people hold tension in their lower back and sacral area, which keeps their pelvis immobile while walking. If your pelvis isn't allowed to rotate, your legs have to work much harder when you walk. This simple focus will turn any walk into a relaxation exercise for your back.

- Another side effect of a "frozen pelvis" is sore hips. This happens because the impact of your foot hitting the ground is taken by your hip joint instead of being cushioned by the softening motion of a rotating pelvis. In chapter 6, I'll take you through some great exercises that loosen your hips and pelvis. I suggest starting every walk with some hip looseners if your pelvis is tight, which is true for most people.

In review, here are the main points to remember when you're practicing your ChiWalking technique.

1. Allow yourself to be drawn forward by the pull of gravity, instead of pushing yourself forward with the thrust of your legs.

2. Don't lock your knees as you swing your legs forward. Keep your knees bent as you swing them forward. This allows your foot to land underneath you instead of out in front of you.

3. Roll forward off the balls of your feet, lifting your knees forward without pushing off. Again, allow gravity to move you forward.

4. Swing your elbows to the rear as a counterbalance to your forward lean, instead of swinging your arms forward while walking.

5. Tilt your statue while walking, instead of maintaining an upright posture. This allows gravity to pull you forward with each step.

6. Swing your arms faster and let your cadence increase as you walk faster. Keep your stride length consistent at all speeds.

7. Allow your spine to twist and your pelvis to rotate while you walk. This keeps the spine healthy and massages all of your internal organs with each step. This will create smoothness in your gait.

8. Hold your pelvis level and don't lead with your hips as you walk. This will reduce pressure on your lower back.

Don't feel pressured to learn the ChiWalking technique all at once. Just practice one focus at a time until you feel comfortable enough to add on another. Allow yourself to build slowly. It will be much easier to learn the complete technique. As you practice each of these focuses one at a time, you'll see them begin to flow together into one coherent movement. If you're more of a visual learner or if you would like to have a clear picture of how ChiWalking is done, I recommend ordering the ChiWalking DVD and using it as a backup for this book.

It is so worth it to make these changes in how you walk because what you get back will help you in every aspect of your life. This walking technique will enhance your walking program whether you're a beginning walker or a seasoned veteran, because your movement will be in alignment with the laws of Nature and the flow of chi. As with any truly mindful practice, the more consistently and constantly you practice the principles of ChiWalking, the deeper your experience will be. Your time will be well spent and you'll begin to reap the benefits immediately.

CHAPTER FIVE

The ChiWalking Menu

There is more to life than increasing its speed.
—GANDHI

H ave you ever wished that there was a way you could change how you're feeling by simply flicking a switch? Like when you've had a lousy night's sleep and you've got to be in an important meeting as soon as you get to work. Or you've had a totally crazy, chaotic day and the last thing you want to do is pick up a carful of kids who are waiting for you to take them to an after-school soccer game.

How do you get energy when you need it, without the use of stimulants?

What can you do to relax yourself when it's what you need most?

How can you get a great workout when you have only 20 minutes?

Once you have familiarized yourself with the basic ChiWalking technique, you'll be ready to open the door to a whole new realm of walking enjoyment. This chapter presents a full spectrum of walks that work on all four levels of the human experience: physical, emotional, mental, and spiritual.

The ChiWalking Menu gives you a list of twelve different walks from which to choose when you feel there's a certain type of energy that you need in your life. From conditioning your body to relaxing your muscles, from calming your heart to sharpening your mind, there's a walk here to help you get what you need. You are about to be introduced to the expanded world of walking, where you can become the master of your body and not a slave to it.

I suggest reading through the list of walks, picking one that resonates with you, then giving it a try. To get a good sense of what each walk can do for you, it's best to practice each of them a few times so that you can get comfortable with what to do. To get a companion audio program, visit www.chiwalking.com.

At the beginning of each walk description there is an overview that states the purpose of the walk, the target heart rate range (listed as a percentage of your maximum heart rate, MHR), cadence ranges (measured in strides per minute, spm), and a suggested length of time you can expect to be out walking.

Since every body is different, we suggest that you consult with your health practitioner before embarking on any workout program.

How to Figure Your Maximum Heart Rate (MHR)

To figure out what your approximate maximum heart rate is, just subtract your age from the number 220. So if you're 50 years old, your maximum heart rate would be $220 - 50 = 170$ beats per minute (bpm). That's approximately the fastest your heart can safely beat. In other words, there is no reason on planet Earth that you should ever want to see your heart rate that high. To figure out what your aerobic heart rate range should be, multiply your maximum heart rate (MHR) by .55 and then by .70. So, $170 \times .55 = 94$ and $170 \times .7 = 119$. Therefore, if you're 50 years old, your aerobic heart rate zone should range between 94 and 119 bpm.

If you're not a math whiz and don't particularly care to do all the figuring, there's another way. If you can walk and sing, you're walking too slowly for an aerobic fitness walk. If you can walk and carry on a conversation without disrupting your sentences, you're probably in the right range. But if you have trouble talking and completing long sentences because you're gasping for air, you've reached your upper limit. Your aerobic zone is where you want your heart rate to be whenever you're out doing any form of aerobic fitness walking.

How to Measure Your Heart Rate: Beats per Minute (bpm)

Your heart rate is measured in beats per minute (bpm), and here are a couple of ways to measure your pulse. The first method is low tech and the least expensive.

1. Hold two fingers at the side of your neck next to your Adam's apple. Count your pulse for 15 seconds and multiply by 4 to get beats per minute.
2. Wear a heart rate monitor, available on our website or at any sporting goods store. These nifty devices will give you a heart rate readout every three seconds and will constantly keep you informed as to exactly what the old ticker is doing.

How to Measure Your Strides per Minute (spm)

This one is pretty simple to do. Just count the number of strides you take with your right leg in 1 minute. That's your strides per minute or spm. The even easier way is to use a metronome and walk with your regular stride and adjust the metronome's beep to each footfall.

All of these walks are listed in the ChiWalking Matrix (see page 137).

1. The Cardio Walk

- Purpose: Strengthens your heart
- Target heart rate range: 70 percent to 80 percent MHR (maximum heart rate)

- Cadence: 70 to 80 spm, alternate fast/easy paces
- Duration: 30 to 45 minutes

WHAT DOES THIS WALK DO?

This walk is specifically devoted to making your heart stronger. And for that reason we suggest that you consult with your doctor before embarking on this or any cardiovascular workout.

When you alternately increase and decrease your heart rate, it strengthens your heart muscle in much the same way that lifting weights with your arms builds strong arm muscles. To get stronger arm muscles, you might start off with a 5-pound weight and lift it 10 times in a set and do 5 sets. Then, over the period of a few weeks you would gradually increase the number of sets of repetitions until the 5-pound weight feels like nothing. Then you'd switch to a 10-pound weight and go back to your original 5 sets of 10 reps, going through the same building process again at the new weight. In this way you gradually get stronger muscles over time. And the slow progression means it feels relatively easy to do.

In this walk, you'll be warming up for 10 minutes at a 60 to 65 spm cadence and then begin your intervals. An interval is a short period of time where you walk fast enough to elevate your heart rate to the high end of your aerobic capacity, followed by a brief time of restful walking where you allow your heart rate to fall back down to the low end of the aerobic scale. Increasing and decreasing your heart rate in this way will build strength in your heart muscle, allowing it to pump blood more efficiently.

WHAT TO DO

Start your walk with an easy 10-minute warm-up walk. Your cadence should be about 60 spm. Once you feel loose and your muscles are warmed up, you'll be starting your intervals. Walk at a very brisk pace for 1 minute and then rest at a mellow pace (60 spm) for 1 minute. Alternate between a minute of fast walking and a minute of slow walking for 10 to 15 minutes and then drop back down to an easy pace to finish the last 10 minutes of your walk.

Whenever you're walking for cardiovascular training, your range will be 60 percent to 85 percent of your maximum heart rate. Using our previous 50-year-old example, your cardiovascular zone will be 102 to 145 bpm depending on your level of conditioning. Because this is an elevated heart rate, you would walk only for short periods at this pace. As you become more fit, your body will be able to safely handle a higher heart rate during exercise.

This walk will be done in intervals, which allow your heart to go through alternating cycles of work and rest—just the right thing for building a strong "muscle."

THE "WORK" INTERVAL

Your cardio minutes will be walked at a brisk pace, which means a high rate of cadence—at least 70 spm. If you have a metronome, set it for 70 to 80 bpm and let it guide your cadence during the "work" intervals. (Small metronomes for walking are available on our Web site; see appendix.) To get your cadence faster during the "work" intervals, you'll need to swing your arms vigorously. Keep your stride short so that your legs can turn over quickly and elevate your heart rate. Bend your arms at a 90-degree angle and swing your elbows vigorously (70 to 80 spm) to the rear as you keep your upper body slightly forward, over your feet. As your heart gets stronger from doing these intervals, you can increase your cadence toward the high end of the range.

THE "REST" INTERVAL

During your rest interval, lower your arms and relax your lean. Let your cadence drop to a comfortable pace (60 to 65 spm), but not all the way down to a leisurely stroll. When you're doing a rest interval, just slow your cadence down to a comfortable recovery pace. Most walkers naturally settle in at about a 60 spm walk. You shouldn't need a metronome for your "rest" intervals if you just do it by "feel," where your breathing slows to the point where you can comfortably carry on a conversation.

HOW OFTEN AND HOW MUCH TO DO

This walk should be done once a week, preferably on the same day. Count the number of work intervals you do each week and keep track of them in a journal so that you can monitor your progress. If you don't want to count each interval, simply take the total number of minutes you were doing the fast/slow intervals and divide by 2. This will give you your number of intervals. Then week by week you can add more intervals as you feel ready.

The best way to tell what number you should be doing is to Body Sense what you're feeling during your later intervals. If you're beginning to feel fatigued and not as capable of holding a brisk cadence, it's time to stop for the day. Make a note of how many you do and try to do at least that same number the following week. Then, when you reach that same number the following week, ask yourself how your body would feel if you added one more interval to the program. If your body doesn't complain very loudly, you're ready for another. But if it seems like it could be an effort to do, wait until next week and try it again.

Never increase your interval numbers if your body is resistant to doing so. Nobody needs to get injured. Remember, we're here to get healthy.

If you do it right, this walk will leave you pleasantly fatigued and invigorated. You'll know you did a workout.

2. The Aerobic Walk

- Purpose: Improves aerobic capacity and metabolizes fat
- Target heart rate range: 55 percent to 70 percent MHR
- Cadence: 60 to 70 spm, moderate pace
- Duration: 60 minutes plus

WHAT DOES THIS WALK DO?

The aerobic walk is a wonderful way to spend time with a friend, catching up on news while keeping your heart, lungs, and legs in great shape. The aerobic walk is a favorite among ChiWalkers because it burns fat and calories. It's one of those great activities that is both fun and healthy.

Is there a catch? You bet. All of the great benefits of the aerobic walk really begin to kick in *after* the first 30 minutes. This means that the longer you're out there, the more efficiently you'll be burning calories. For this reason, your aerobic walks should generally be your longest walks. If you're not used to walking for more than 30 minutes, work your way up to 30 and then extend that base either weekly or bi-weekly. Whenever you extend any type of walk, do it in minutes, not miles. A 5-minute upgrade once a week is plenty. In no time you'll be up to walking an hour without thinking twice.

Bear in mind that this walk is not intended to build leg strength or cardiovascular fitness per se. It is designed to improve your oxygen transport systems so that your lungs work more efficiently and your muscles are well oxygenated during exercise. Therefore, we recommend doing this walk at an easy, comfortable pace. If you walk too fast during an aerobic walk, you'll burn through your muscle glycogen too quickly, which will leave you feeling hungry afterward and craving the carbohydrates needed to replace your muscle glycogen.

If, instead, you walk at a comfortable pace within your aerobic zone, your body will sense the difference and will burn glycogen at a much slower rate. After approximately 30 minutes, your body will begin to burn fat cells (instead of primarily glycogen) for power. Glycogen is utilized during the fat-burning process, but at a very slow rate.

It is crucial to keep your pace comfortable during this walk because the faster you walk, the more glycogen you burn—and the less fat you burn. So if you want to burn the maximum fat per minute of exercise, keep your aerobic walks at 55 percent to 70 percent MHR, depending on your level of conditioning, and work up to walking for 30 minutes or more. If you walk for 1 hour your body will burn 50 percent fat and 50 percent glycogen. That figure changes to about 70 percent fat/30 percent glycogen after 2 hours and a very generous 80 percent fat/20 percent glycogen after 3 hours. See? Sometimes it pays to go slow.

- Warm-up: 10 minutes
- Cadence: 60 to 65 spm
- Long slow distance
- It's not a race, but it is consistent
- Hold cadence for longer periods of time

- Conversational, but just
- Heart rate should be 55 percent to 70 percent MHR
- Arms half-bent
- Build up to 1 hour

HOW DO I DO IT?

The terrain doesn't matter as long as you can keep a steady pace and you're not having to stop often. Your arms will be half-bent and your cadence will be 60 to 65 spm. Your stride should feel comfortable— not too slow but not too fast either. Try to keep your cadence between 60 and 70 spm. Keep your heart rate within your aerobic zone, which is 55 percent to 70 percent of your maximum heart rate.

HOW MUCH

This is one of the most enjoyable and most beneficial walks you can do. If you're just beginning a walking program, start with 30 minutes and work your way up to where you're able to walk for 1 hour. Once you're up to an hour, the sky's the limit, but increase at a safe rate: no more than 10 percent increase in overall time per week.

3. THE HILLY WALK

- Purpose: Building upper-body and leg strength
- Target heart rate range: 60 percent to 75 percent MHR
- Cadence: 60 to 70 spm, moderate pace
- Duration: 30 to 45 minutes (or more if desired)

I can't help it, I'm partial to hills. I love walking the trails near my home every chance I get. I think of it as three-dimensional walking, where I'm not just turning left or right, but adding in those wonderful components of up and down also. Even a little elevation gain allows views to open up, and there is some amount of comfort I derive from knowing where I am relative to my surroundings. I feel fortunate indeed to live in an area with endless hills and beautiful vistas. But even if you happen to live in an area that is flat, you'll always encounter hills at some point whenever you travel. So this walk could

eventually apply to you too. You can also use the focuses for this walk
if you're on a treadmill set at an incline.

WHAT DOES THIS WALK DO?

This workout will accomplish a few things. You will build your
upper- and lower-body muscles, especially those in your hips and
shoulders. You'll learn the value of good consistent pacing and how
you can use your technique to make *any* hill seem easy. And walking hills is always a prime opportunity to get a great cardio-aerobic
workout.

HOW DO I DO IT?

Trails are ideal, but a hilly neighborhood works just as well. If you're
unfamiliar with where the hills are near your home, you can always
ask a friend if he or she has any favorite hilly places to recommend. I
also like to bike to nearby hills. This gives my legs a nice warm-up on
the way to my walk.

Dress in layers. There is generally more exertion involved with
hiking hills, so your body temperature can go through a wide range
during the course of a walk. When you're walking uphill you'll get
warm, but as soon as you head back down again your body will cool off
and you'll wish you had that sweater you left in the car. If I'm going
very far, I'll wear a small day pack so that I can carry everything I
might need: clothing, food, and water. To avoid overstretching your
legs at the beginning of your walk, warm up in a flat area for 5 to 10
minutes before heading up into the hills.

On the uphills, your stride should be a little shorter than it is
when you're walking on the flats, and your cadence will be slower
when you're climbing. Depending on the steepness of the grade
you're climbing it could vary between 55 and 70 spm but not much
faster than that. The important thing to remember is to settle into a
comfortable cadence and walk steadily at that pace. If you start and
stop a lot, or if your cadence varies too much, you'll burn your energy
at an uneven rate, which is inefficient and a lot more tiring.

Steady is the key word here. When climbing steep grades, the main
thrust of your legs will come from the swing of your pelvis and the

Figure 34a—Lean forward, reach up the hill with your arm swing, and straighten your rear leg

Figure 34b—Incorrect uphill technique: stride is too long and body is too upright

straightening of your rear leg with each step. Don't step up the hill ahead of yourself and pull yourself up with your legs or you could be in for a hamstring injury. Always lean up the hill so that your upper body remains directly over your feet as they come down onto the ground. As soon as your foot touches the ground, drive with your hip and straighten your leg.

When walking uphill, your arm swing will be a very full swing, even exaggerated. Unlike your arm swing on level ground (where your arms always swing to the rear) your arm swing on the uphills will swing fully forward as if you're pulling yourself up with a rope and also fully to the rear. Each time you drive with your hip and leg, you'll be reaching up the hill with one arm while you're reaching toward the back with your opposite elbow.

When you're walking downhill, keep your knees bent at all times and shorten your stride to reduce impact. It also helps to tuck your tailbone; this flattens your lower back and reduces any stress that can occur there.

HOW MUCH DO I DO?

For your hilly walk you can stay out as long as feels comfortable. Generally a walk of this nature can be one of your longer walks, so the range can be from 45 minutes to over an hour. Just Body Sense what feels right. Doing a hilly walk will work your body harder than a flat walk, so when you think about how far to go, the rule is: don't walk farther on a hilly walk than you would on a flat walk. This way you'll keep your distance within a safe range.

Here are a couple of other hill workouts that will increase your cardiovascular fitness and help strengthen your hips and shoulders.

Hill Intervals

Find a hill that is roughly a block long or 2 minutes of uphill walking. It can be steep or shallow depending on your level of conditioning. Obviously, the steeper the hill, the more strenuous the workout. As your cardiovascular conditioning improves, you should graduate yourself to steeper hills for your interval workouts.

Warm up in a flat area at least 10 minutes before starting your intervals. Start at the bottom of the hill and keep a brisk cadence (65 to 70 spm) and a longer-than-normal stride using the technique tips I mentioned above. Lean into the hill and exaggerate your hip swing and arm swing.

When you get to the top (or walk for 2 minutes), turn around and walk back down the hill with short brisk steps, picking up your feet as you go. Your cadence could get as high as 75 to 80 spm depending on the steepness of the hill—the steeper the hill, the faster your cadence will be. Shorten your arm swing on the downhill section. Then, when you get back to the bottom of the hill, turn around and head up for another interval.

The Duration Hill Walk

This walk is done at a cadence range of 60 to 70 spm and on a shallower grade than the hill intervals. The theme of this walk is consistency. Try to keep a consistent cadence and stride length while walking up a long hill. The idea is to regulate your speed so that your effort level remains consistent throughout the length of the hill. Your goal should be to sense the same perceived rate of exertion at the top as you did at the bottom.

HOW MUCH DO I DO?

Do as many as feel comfortable without overexerting yourself. If you feel any discomfort in your chest or difficulty breathing, stop your intervals immediately, allow yourself to recover, and head back down the hill slowly.

This walk is designed to strengthen your heart, not to overwork it, so be careful and Body Sense what your limits are. Make note of how many intervals you were able to do, so that the next time you'll have a number at which to start. We recommend doing this workout weekly because it provides great cardiovascular conditioning and muscle strength.

The hill should preferably be a consistent incline, longer than a half mile if you can find a suitable one. The conditioning from this workout will really pay off when you're out on long hikes that involve miles of steady climbing. Your total walking time can be anywhere from 30 minutes to 1 hour.

If you're training for a walking event that is on a hilly course, find a hill in your area that is a "mockup" of the longest hill climb in the event. Then practice walking that hill until you can cover the climb comfortably and with a consistent heart rate.

Either of these hill walks will get your heart rate into your upper aerobic zones and improve your cardiovascular fitness level.

4. THE LOOSENING WALK

- **Purpose:** Loosening your muscles and joints while relaxing your entire body
- **Target heart rate range:** 50 percent to 65 percent MHR
- **Cadence:** 55 to 65 spm, very easy pace
- **Duration:** 30 to 45 minutes

WHAT DOES THIS WALK DO?

When you find yourself holding lots of tension in your body, this walk will work wonders to loosen your muscles and joints, leaving you feeling like you just had a great massage. It's a good walk if you've been sitting in a car or an airplane for hours on end. As soon as possible after traveling, treat yourself to a loosening walk and you'll be back to normal before you know it.

HOW DO I DO IT?

During this walk you'll be walking at a relaxed pace while doing a series of loosening exercises that focus on specific areas of your body.

Before starting your walk, stand in place and shake your whole body. Let your arms dangle and shake your hips and spine so that your body jiggles all over. This will help to release some tension in your muscles right from the start.

Begin walking at an easy pace. During this walk you'll be starting with your head and working your way down your body to your feet.

1. Loosen your face. Tense all the muscles in your face for 5 seconds and then relax and let them go. Do this for 1 minute.
2. Loosen your neck. Do 5 neck rolls (tilting your head around in a circle) in one direction and then 5 in the opposite direction. They don't have to be big circles—any amount of neck roll helps. Keep alternating neck rolls in both directions for 1 minute.
3. Loosen your shoulders. Roll one shoulder at a time in a big circular motion (forward, upward, rearward, and down) until it comes back to its neutral position. Do 5 shoulder rolls on one side and

then do 5 more with the opposite shoulder. Alternate back and forth for 1 minute.

4. Loosen your arms. Dangle your arms at your sides and let them go totally limp while you shake your wrists. This will loosen and relax all the muscles up and down your arms. Do this for 1 minute.

5. Loosen your spine. Bend your elbows to 90 degrees and hold them tightly against your sides (don't let your arms swing). Hold your upper body motionless and let your lower body rotate fully with each stride. You'll feel a slight twist along your spine as you walk this way. This twisting motion will loosen up all the ligaments and tendons along your spine, so really allow the twist to happen. Walk for 1 minute feeling the twist of your spine and then relax your arms, letting them swing normally again.

6. Loosen your hips and pelvis. Every time your leg swings toward the back, allow your hip to go back with it. This motion will increase the rotation of your pelvis and allow your hips to increase their range of motion. You'll feel like you're taking giant steps. Do this for 1 minute.

7. Shorten your stride and walk with your lower legs totally limp. Just pick your feet up off the ground with each step and you'll be able to keep your calves and ankles relaxed throughout each stride. Soften your feet with each footfall. Walk this way for 1 minute.

HOW MUCH?

Cycle through the focuses of each body section in 1-minute intervals and then start over again at the top and work your way to your feet. In a 30-minute walk you'll be able to do four cycles.

This is a good walk even if you have only 15 minutes to spare. It's also a great walk to do as the beginning of a longer walk. Try it for a lunchtime break and you'll come back to your desk refreshed, relaxed, and ready for a calm afternoon of work.

5. The Upper-Body Walk

- Purpose: Strengthening and toning your shoulders and arms
- Target heart rate range: 55 percent to 70 percent MHR
- Cadence: 65 to 70 spm, moderate pace
- Duration: 30 to 45 minutes

WHAT DOES THIS WALK DO?

If you're feeling a bit wimpy in your arms, chest, or shoulders, you'll love this walk. It will strengthen and tone the muscles in your shoulders and arms. It involves carrying small handheld weights while you're walking at an aerobic pace. Find weights that are comfortable and compact, and that have a hand strap that allows you to relax your grip while walking.

HOW DO I DO IT?

1. Do your normal 10-minute warm-up and settle into a 60 to 65 spm pace.
2. Holding the hand weights, bend your elbows to 90 degrees and swing your arms with your palms facing down.
3. Rotate your hands to where your palms are facing toward each other (normal walking position) and walk.
4. Swing your arms with your palms facing up as you walk.
5. Straighten your arms and let them swing at your sides with the hand weights. Keep your elbows straight while swinging your arms and you'll get a great shoulder workout. Start out with a small range of motion and increase the range of swing as your shoulders can handle more.

Here are a few suggestions for additional intervals if you want more of a workout.

- Hold your arms straight out at your sides (like you're an airplane) and walk for 5 minutes.
- Hold your arms straight out in front of you while you walk for 5 minutes.

- Raise and lower your arms at your sides (like you're flapping your wings) for 5 minutes.
- While keeping your elbows at your sides, alternate bending your elbows with each step (curls).

HOW MUCH DO I DO?

Each of the exercises above can be done for 5-minute intervals or until your muscles begin to feel fatigued, whichever comes first. It is crucial during this workout to Body Sense your limits so that you don't overwork any of your muscles. As your body gets used to the workload, you can increase the length of the intervals. This workout can be 30 to 45 minutes. Stretch well afterward.

You might feel some muscle soreness for a day or two after this workout, which is fine. Drink plenty of fluids to flush all the lactic acid out of your muscles.

6. THE CHI-GATHERING WALK

- Purpose: Gathering chi energy into your body
- Target heart rate range: 50 percent to 65 percent MHR
- Cadence: 55 to 65 spm, very slow pace
- Duration: 60 minutes plus

This walk works to stimulate your senses, allowing you to take in more chi from the world around you.

Chi is the energy that you perceive and take in through your senses. It is the energy that connects you with the outer world. When you see a beautiful view and feel good from it, you could say that that site had lots of chi. Eckhart Tolle says of chi, "It is the life within every form, the inner essence of all that exists."

WHAT DOES THIS WALK DO?

In this walk we'll work on developing our senses and on gathering the chi from the world around us and using it to fuel our health, vitality, and daily activities.

The key to this walk is to Body Sense, of course, and to close off your mind to all extraneous thinking and focus entirely on your senses. You will be listening to, looking at, and feeling your sense impressions with as much focus and single-minded attention as you can.

The best place to do this kind of walk is in Nature, to whatever extent you can. The deeper in Nature, and the more remote from other people and the trappings of civilization, the better (keeping safety in mind). The chi in Nature is the purest and best form of chi to gather. It is in Nature that chi is most abundant and most powerful.

SET UP THE RIGHT CONDITIONS

Allow yourself plenty of time on both ends of this walk. It's ideal if you can devote an entire morning to this walk so that you don't feel rushed anywhere in the process. Leave your cell phone, your thoughts, and your agendas at home. Pick a day on which the weather won't be a problem. You don't want rain, snow, or anything else to dampen your day. After you've done this walk a number of times, you can invite a friend along, but otherwise we strongly suggest doing it alone and even in a place in Nature where you won't be disturbed.

Since the object of this walk is to work with impressions, don't worry about how far or fast you go. In fact, this walk is done at such a slow rate that it might not be considered real exercise. Even though I mentioned that you should allow a half day for this walk, you probably won't end up going very far. I've had chi-gathering walks that lasted 3 to 4 hours but covered only a mile. Rest assured that what you will come away with goes so far beyond walking that the trade-off is well worth it.

WHAT TO BRING

- A day pack and water
- Hot tea in a thermos bottle if you have one (not necessary, but a very nice addition to the day)
- A small camping pad or yoga mat to sit on
- Any clothing you might need in case of a change in weather

WHERE TO GO

Pick a spot ahead of time. If a park is as close to Nature as you can get, then go there. You won't be walking far, but you do want an area that you can explore a bit. Choose your very favorite spot for this walk, where you enjoy the scenery and feel relaxed. Some suggestions are: parks, nature preserves, or a beach (where you can walk barefoot, if you like).

HOW DO I DO IT?:
THE CHI-GATHERING MOVEMENTS

This set of movements will also act to prepare you and help you take in chi. Follow the gestures in figures 35a through 35i. They're simple but powerful and will allow you to fully engage your senses during your walk. Once you practice following the step-by-step directions, you want to make the total movement fluid and each successive step flow into the next. I have named the steps so that you can visualize what each one is doing.

1. **Stand in the Grounding Stance** (exhale and bend your knees). Feel the earth underneath you, supporting your body.
2. **Open your doors** (inhale and straighten your knees). Rotate your wrists as you cross your arms in front of your body, raising them up until they are extended straight up over your head. Breathe in the chi around you.
3. **Sink into the earth** (exhale and bend your knees). Lower your arms down, keeping your palms facing forward.

Figure 35a—Begin with the Grounding Stance

Figure 35b—Cross your arms while raising them, palms facing outward

Figure 35c—Open your arms and let the chi in

Figure 35d—Sink into the earth

Figure 35e—Reach down for the chi

Figure 35g—Raise your elbows and put a lid on your container

Figure 35f—Bend your arms to gather up the chi

Figure 35h—Push the chi down into your belly

Figure 35i—Return to the Grounding Stance

4. **Gather the chi into your chest** (inhale and straighten your knees). Bend your elbows and bring your hands up until your palms are facing your chest.

5. **Put a lid on your container.** Let your elbows swing up at your sides until your arms are horizontal and your middle fingers are touching.

6. **Push the chi down into your belly** (exhale and bend your knees). Push down with your hands until your arms are extended down in front of your body as in the starting position.

7. **Repeat** steps 1 through 6 for 5 minutes.

You'll notice that every time your knees bend, you exhale, and every time they straighten, you inhale. Once you get the hang of this exercise, you'll find it to be one of the most relaxing and focusing exercises you'll ever do. Trust us on this one.

After 5 minutes of this exercise, you're ready to begin your walk.

THE CHI-GATHERING WALK

The point of this walk is to feed your senses on all that is delightful. This is not a linear walk where you're going from point A to point B, but instead, a walk where you follow whatever draws your attention. As you stroll along, let your eyes rest on whatever is of interest. You can let yourself go into the tiny details or the big vista, it doesn't matter. There is no right or wrong, just what is appealing, beautiful, or important to you. It may be the pattern in the bark of a tree, or the details of a flower, or the shape of a curve in the stream. You can stop and fully enjoy anything you'd like. The point here is to take the time to let your senses guide you. Listen to the sounds, look at the colors and shapes, feel the breeze or the ground underfoot, smell the aromas. Let your senses come fully alive.

Here are some tips for making your walk a truly nourishing experience:

- Move slowly.
- Don't explain or label anything, just watch.
- You don't have to always be moving. If you feel like stopping or pausing, go ahead.
- Let your eyes watch in three dimensions. Notice how some things are closer and some things are farther away. This will help to break your eyes away from the habit of seeing the world as a flat canvas.
- As you walk, be aware of all your senses working one at a time. Cycle through each of your senses at first, then work to gradually have an awareness of all of them working at once.
- Instead of seeing everything through the eyes in your head, pretend you have eyes in your chest and that all the impressions you're taking in are coming directly in through your chest, not necessarily through your eyes. This allows the impressions coming in to have a deeper effect on you than merely visual.

Spend as much time as you wish walking in this manner: stopping, starting, pausing, watching, relaxing, and simply feasting on everything around you.

When you feel satiated, walk back to your starting point and repeat the beginning set of gestures for a couple of minutes before continuing on with your day. The idea is to take with you as much of the chi you just gathered as possible. Before you move on, Body Sense. How does your body feel? Do you sense energy in your body? You want to bring that energy with you into whatever you do next.

As you bring this walk into your life, maybe once a month if possible, you'll get better and better at opening your body and your senses and at gathering the chi from the world around you.

You can use this anytime to gather energy when you need it. All your walks can take on the added benefit of gathering chi while you walk. If you have a long walking event planned, such as a long hike or a walkathon, this walk will be a great source of energizing fuel for you to tap into.

7. THE GROUNDING WALK

- Purpose: Collecting yourself when you're feeling scattered and "outside" of yourself
- Target heart rate range: 50 percent to 65 percent MHR
- Cadence: 55 to 65 spm, very easy pace
- Duration: 30 to 45 minutes

WHAT DOES THIS WALK DO?

This walk is great for when you're feeling scattered and outside of yourself—like you don't quite have a handle on your life. When I find myself in this state, it is very predictable where most of my energy can be found. It's in my head. That's right. And when I'm there, I'm not in my body. There's nothing worse than being stuck in your head without any chance of escape.

This Grounding Walk will help you to move all of the extra energy in your head by directing it down into the lower regions of your body. When your energy is stuck "upstairs," the most important thing you can do for yourself is to place your mental focus as far from your brain as possible. For this reason, all of the focused attention during this walk will be below your waist. You'll be paying close attention to your pelvis, legs, and feet.

HOW DO I DO IT?

As with any walk where you're directing your energy, this walk begins with a Grounding Stance. Take a few minutes at the beginning to get into the stance and feel your feet underneath you supporting your posture line. Your pelvis should be level, held in place by your lower abdominal muscles. This will serve to gather energy to your center and away from your head. Body Sense your legs supporting your pelvis and your feet supporting your legs.

Begin walking at a pace that is comfortable and slightly on the slow side. Walk with your knees slightly bent at all times. Move along quietly and softly on your feet, like you're trying to sneak up on somebody. Allow yourself to sink into the earth more than usual. Feel yourself moving smoothly across the surface of the earth like you're on a conveyor belt.

After a few minutes of walking, once you're into a nice comfortable walk, do this: Every time your heel comes down onto the ground, feel the connection between your body and the earth. Let the energy from your hips and pelvis drop down into the ground with each heel strike. Then as you roll onto the balls of your feet, feel the chi from the earth come back up through your legs and return to your hips and pelvis. This will create a continuous cycle of energy moving down from your pelvis to your feet and then returning back to your pelvis.

Allow yourself plenty of time to focus on cycling energy through the lower half of your body. This will effectively redirect the energy in your head to a new location, leaving you clearheaded and able to regain the upper hand on the chaos in your mind.

HOW MUCH DO I DO?

The length of time you do this walk is totally up to you. If you're feeling scattered and outside of yourself, you can do it until you feel a clear sense of collectedness and ease returning to your body.

This walk is convenient because you can do it anytime and anywhere you feel the need to get out of your head. Now, no matter what the circumstances, you can always get grounded, centered, and more settled into yourself simply by pulling this walk out of your bag of tricks.

8. The Energizing Walk

- Purpose: Increasing the flow of chi through your body
- Target heart rate range: 60 percent to 70 percent MHR
- Cadence: 60 to 70 spm, moderate pace
- Duration: 30 to 45 minutes

WHAT DOES THIS WALK DO?

This walk is useful for getting your energy moving when you feel that your body is in a low-energy phase. If you're feeling tired or lethargic, it doesn't necessarily mean that you don't have any energy. It means that your energy is stagnant and not moving. Through the use of breath work and visualization, this walk will leave you feeling refreshed and invigorated with your chi flowing once again.

HOW DO I DO IT?

One of the main things you'll be focusing on during this walk is your breath. You'll be belly breathing as fully and as often as you can. I'll review the belly-breathing focuses that were mentioned earlier in this book.

Begin by forcing all the air out of your lungs by pulling in on your belly while blowing out through your pursed lips. When you've fully emptied your lungs, relax your abdominals and allow your belly to expand, filling your lungs from the bottom. Once your belly is fully expanded, allow your chest to expand to complete the breath—then go back through the cycle over and over again. Before you take off on your walk do a couple of minutes of belly breathing so that it will be in your body consciousness when you start walking.

1. Start walking at a relaxed pace; 60 to 70 strides per minute is a good cadence. You should be moving at what feels like a moderate pace. Do your belly breathing throughout the entire walk. Breathe fully and slowly with each breath, making sure that your lungs completely empty and completely fill with each breath cycle.

2. Walk for 5 minutes doing belly breathing and then begin this energetic visualization: Imagine a stream of energy rising up

the back side of your spine each time you inhale. It flows from your tailbone to the top of your head. Then when you exhale, imagine the same stream of energy flowing back down the front side of your spine all the way to your pubic bone. When you inhale again, the stream of energy will again rise to the top of your head and flow back down with your out breath. Keep this breathing-visualizing cycle going for the entire length of your walk.

This walk is best done alone so that you can just be with your mental focus and your breath without interruption.

HOW MUCH DO I DO?

The length of this walk ranges from 20 minutes to an hour depending on how much energy you need. The more you can belly breathe and clearly visualize the energy moving up and down through your body, the more effective this walk will be.

This is a very powerful exercise for getting your chi to flow, so it shouldn't be done right before bedtime. Rather, aim for first thing in the morning, after you wake up. It can easily energize you for a whole day. It is also a great walk to do in the late afternoon when your energy is starting to lag. Take a 15-minute break and go outside for an energizing walk. It's like giving yourself a "chi zap."

9. The Focusing Walk

- Purpose: Focusing and relaxing your mind
- Target heart rate range: 60 percent to 70 percent MHR
- Cadence: 60 to 70 spm, very easy pace
- Duration: 30 to 45 minutes

WHAT DOES THIS WALK DO?

Here's a walk that is more for your brain than your body, and that's a good thing. How many activities do you do in a day that help you to think better while relaxing your mind at the same time? Learning to focus your mind is one of the best skills you can acquire. It can help you to better utilize your mind in your everyday activities and keep you sharp and clearheaded in your later years.

Although it might sound counterintuitive, focusing your mind is actually a way to rest your brain. There are literally hundreds of thoughts that float through our brains every minute. They're mostly unconscious, associative thoughts that fill up our idle time. Daydreaming, phantom conversations, songs, to-do lists—the stream of unconsciousness goes on mostly uninterrupted all day long. By the time we finish a full day of such random undirected thought, we're wiped out from overthinking.

When you focus your mind, you're giving it only one thing to do, and that singular thought can replace all the myriad other thoughts that would like to crowd onto center stage. It is very restful for the mind to follow only one thought at a time. It's similar to the effect that meditation has on the brain. When your thoughts are simpler, your brain waves become more orderly and rhythmic, "resting" the brain from the work of daily details. In this walk I will present a number of focuses to do while walking. Any one of them will help you to focus and quiet your mind. I strongly suggest doing this walk once a week, especially if your job demands that you frequently work with lots of details.

HOW DO I DO IT?

Everyone has different needs when it comes to focusing and resting their mind, so play with these walks and customize them to fit your needs if necessary. Anything that helps to rest your mind by eliminating extraneous thinking is good.

Focus Walk 1: Eyes on the Horizon

Find a place to walk that is flat with few obstructions. A good clean sidewalk or bike path is great. Start walking at a relaxed pace. Your cadence should be around 60 to 65 spm. Once you're settled into your cadence, look ahead of you into the distance and pick something on which to focus. It can be anything—a tree, a telephone pole, a parked car. It doesn't matter, as long as it's far enough ahead that you can keep your gaze on it for at least a minute. When you've picked out your object, hold your gaze on it without breaking your visual focus or taking your eyes off it. It might feel a bit awkward at first, but eventually you'll be able to keep your eyes up ahead while being able to see your immediate surroundings with your peripheral vision. When you've walked far enough toward your object of focus that you can no longer use it as a focus, find another object in the distance and switch your focus to that. In this way you'll leapfrog from one focus to the next throughout your entire walk and you'll always have something on which to focus and quiet your mind.

Focus Walk 2: Watch Your Breath

This walk is simple in nature but difficult to do. All you have to do is observe each breath as it enters and leaves your body. Watch yourself inhale . . . and then exhale. Whenever you find your mind drifting to other thoughts, just gently bring it back to watching your breath go in and out.

Challenge yourself with being able to walk for 30 to 45 minutes without missing a breath. When you're able to do it, your victory won't be in the fact that you didn't miss a breath. It will be in the fact that you quieted your mind. You'll be able to feel the spaciousness in your mind when you're done.

Focus Walk 3: Repeating a Sound or Phrase

This particular technique has been used for millennia by spiritual seekers in every culture as a method for quieting and focusing the mind. It involves the use of a sound, a word, or a phrase to calm and center the mind. Hindus might use the word "om," while Sufis use the word "hu." Christians and Jews both say "amen."

Every culture and world religion has a word or phrase that helps one connect more deeply with one's inner self. When you're using a word or phrase with your walking, pick one that resonates with you and use it as a focal point. Here are some suggestions of words and phrases:

"I am here and focused and relaxed."
"My movement is stable and centered."

"My mind is quiet and focused."

"I am here."

Focus Walk 4: The Form Focus Walk

One of the most useful focus walks is when you spend the entire time working on the ChiWalking Form Focuses in 1-minute intervals. Before heading out for your walk, think about which ChiWalking Form Focuses will help you the most to become more efficient with your walking technique. Then set your countdown timer for 1-minute intervals and practice each focus on your list for 1 minute at a time. When your timer goes off, switch to your next focus and do it for the next minute. Cycle through all of the focuses on your list and then begin again. Do this for your entire walk. During each 1-minute interval you should focus *all* of your attention on the focus at hand and not think of anything else. This walk does two jobs in one: it improves your technique while quieting your mind at once. What a deal.

HOW MUCH DO I DO?

These four examples of focusing walks represent four different ways to focus and relax your mind. The first walk uses a visual focus; the second walk uses a physical focus; the third one is a feeling approach; and the fourth one is a mind-body approach. Each is a valid way to accomplish the same goal of having a quiet and rested mind. The ideal time frame for these walks is 30 to 45 minutes.

At the end of your walk, give yourself some time to transition into your next activity. You've just done a lot of work to quiet your mind, so avoid rushing off headlong into your next activity. Move slowly and take the time to appreciate the gift you've just given yourself. You'll be glad you did.

10. THE CALMING WALK

- Purpose: Calming your mind and relaxing your body
- Target heart rate range: 50 percent to 65 percent MHR

- Cadence: 55 to 65 spm, very easy pace
- Duration: 30 to 45 minutes

WHAT DOES IT DO?

You've just had the "day from hell." Your nerves are shot, and there's a steel rod running up and down your spine. Fear not, help is just a few steps away. This walk will help you to pull the plug on all that energy stuck up in your head. You'll learn how to rid yourself of frenetic energy that can throw you off balance and leave you feeling like a pile of nerves. This walk does just what it says. It's a calming walk. So whenever you need to take the edge off and realign yourself with a more sane sense in your body, just give yourself this walk and you'll come back a different person.

This is a perfect walk to practice nose breathing. Breathing in and out through your nose has a very calming effect on your nervous system.

HOW DO I DO IT?

If you have the time to spare, make yourself a cup of tea before heading out for your walk. We suggest decaffeinated herbal tea such as chamomile. You remember. It's the tea that Peter Rabbit's mother gave him after his ordeal with Mr. McGregor. She knew exactly what tea would calm Peter Rabbit and help him recover from his near-death experience. It's a wonderfully calming drink that's good any time you've had a day that needs the corners rounded off a little. Brew yourself a cup and then take a few minutes to sit comfortably and sip while you let all those worries of your day melt away like spring icicles.

When you're done with your tea, get your shoes on and head out for a walk. Start with setting your posture straight so that your energy can flow well while you're walking.

The theme of a calming walk is to do whatever it takes to settle your energy. For most people it's not the energy in their body that needs calming, it's the energy in their head. So the best tactic is to direct your energy downward, away from your head. Begin walking at a very slow and relaxing pace—50 spm should be fine. This is not so much a physical workout as it is a calming and relaxing walk. The emphasis should not be on getting a great physical workout. Save that for another day when you need to get your ya-ya's out. We're calming now.

For this walk, your arms can swing fully extended at your sides in a nice relaxed way. Begin by focusing on your breath. Breathe out for 6 steps and then breathe in for 6 steps. If possible, try to breathe through your nose the entire time. This will stimulate nerve sensors in your nose which work to calm the mind. Here's what osteopath Robert C. Fulford, DO, says in his book *Dr. Fulford's Touch of Life* about nose breathing: "Remember: always try to breathe through your nostrils, and not through your mouth, because air must contact the olfactory nerves to stimulate your brain and put it into its natural rhythm. If you don't breathe through your nose, in a sense you're only half alive."

During your in breath, feel your chest expand with calming energy, and then on your out breath, feel that energy move down your spine and flow into your center, just below your navel. Spend the first 10 minutes of your walk just breathing this way, slowly and deeply through your nose. Feel your feet on the ground with each step. This will help to lower your center of gravity and place your attention away from your head.

Do this walk alone. Carrying on a conversation with a friend while trying to calm yourself is not a good bet for success, because you'll most likely get into talking about whatever it was that made you uptight to begin with and then you'll just be creating more of the energy you're working to calm.

Once you've been walking and breathing fully for 10 minutes, do this: while walking, imagine a waterfall flowing down your spine carrying with it all the tensions of the day. Imagine that it begins at the base of your skull and cascades down to your tailbone, continuously flowing and washing all of the tension out of your body as it flows down your spine. If you find your thoughts wandering, just gently return to what you're doing.

HOW MUCH?

Hold this focus for at least 20 to 30 minutes or for as long as you feel the need. When you're finished with your walk, find a nice spot and take a few minutes to just sit and relax. Remain silent and just watch the world go by. How often do we let ourselves do *this*? Be sure to acknowledge to yourself whatever amount of calm you just produced in your body and mind. This is a very important step to take, because it builds in you a sense that you can and do have control over your anxious moments. With this walk you can neutralize anxiety regularly so that it doesn't get a chance to build up inside.

11. The Walking Meditation

- Purpose: Quieting and focusing the mind
- Target heart rate range: 50 percent to 65 percent MHR
- Cadence: 55 to 65 spm, very slow pace
- Duration: 20 to 30 minutes

WHAT DOES THIS WALK DO?

There are few activities we do in our lives that leave us with a strong sense of centeredness. This walk does just that. Directing your mind to a specific focal point, you'll learn how to create a sense of quiet centeredness in your being.

This walk is similar to a sitting meditation except that you're using movement as a vehicle instead of stillness. It is designed to quiet your mind while creating a sense of stillness within your movement. As you become increasingly adept at this practice, you'll be able to feel your own quiet center inside of you during your everyday activities, and you'll grow from being a centered walker to being a centered person.

Since this is an internal practice, there is less emphasis put on your surroundings. For this reason, you'll be walking in a small contained area to limit distractions from the "outer world." You can use anyplace that allows about 20 to 30 feet of walking in any given stretch. It could be your living room or an area in your backyard—anywhere you can ensure that you won't be disturbed while you're walking.

HOW DO I DO IT?

Pick the spot where you'll be doing your walk. All you'll need is a level straight section of ground about 20 feet long. You'll be walking back and forth from one end of the path to the other for the duration of the walk.

1. Begin your Meditative Walk by doing the Grounding Stance for 2 or 3 minutes (see figures 45a and 45b, pg. 156). When you feel yourself settled into your Grounding Stance, place your attention on the front side of your spine—from the base of the skull to the tailbone. The *front* side of your spine is the deepest area of your body. Visualize it and use that image as a focal point to return to over and over again. This walking meditation is a clear example of the ChiWalking principle of Needle in Cotton. Your spine is your needle, which is surrounded by the rest of your body, the cotton. The "hard focus" is on your spine while the "soft focus" is on the rest of your body.

    Start at the top of your spine and let your attention follow a path down the front of your spine until you reach your tailbone. Then repeatedly go back and start over again from the top. Move your attention slowly as you "scan" your spine. When you find your mind drifting, and it will, just gently remind yourself to return your focus to the area along the front side of your spine.

2. After you've done the Grounding Stance and set up your focus, begin walking very slowly and deliberately, feeling each foot on the ground with every step. Thin-soled shoes work great for this walk. Soften your eyes so that your field of vision is slightly blurred. This will keep visual distraction to a minimum. Keep your posture tall and straight and breathe slowly and deeply. The most important thing to focus on while you're walking is your spine. You can even imagine that you don't have a body—that you're just a spine moving along the path. Allow the rest of your body to disappear into the background of your thoughts and focus on your spine.

3. When you come to the end of your path, stop and slowly turn around, then walk back the length of the path, always returning

your focus to the front of your spine. Keep your eyes from looking around as you turn.

HOW MUCH DO I DO?

The first time you do the Meditative Walk, go for only 10 minutes, just enough time to get a sense of how to do it. Then the next time you do it, you can walk for any amount of time that feels appropriate and complete. This walk can be used any time you feel the need to center yourself, which can be anywhere from daily to weekly.

12. RACEWALKING

Since I am not an expert on the topic of racewalking, I turned to my friend and long-time racewalker Keith McConnell, PhD, to describe to me the ins and outs of this great sport.

The "high" of racing is not limited to only runners. For those of you with a need for speed, there's racewalking. The fast mode of walking has long been included in such events as the Olympics and the World Games. Amazingly, the fastest racewalkers can walk at a pace of 6.5 minutes per mile, faster than most recreational *runners*. They are able to sustain a cadence of 80 strides per minute, where most recreational walkers will range between 70 and 80 spm.

The differences between regular walking and racewalking are small but worth mentioning. In a sanctioned racewalking event, you must follow a couple of basic rules: (1) You can never lose contact with the ground. If you do, you're considered to be running, not walking. (2) Your forward leg must be straight as it makes contact with the ground. If you don't abide by these rules you'll either get disqualified or be given a warning by race monitors.

The interesting thing about racewalking is that it shares many of the same focuses used in ChiWalking. In a nutshell, here are some of the main focuses used in racewalking.

- You use your core muscles instead of relying solely on your leg muscles for propulsion.
- Engaging the pull of gravity with a slight lean is preferred over walking with the upper body held upright.

- Posture and alignment are critical for efficient walking.
- Your stride opens to the rear, not to the front.
- You allow your pelvis to rotate and move freely while you're walking.
- Your arm swing and leg swing have equal importance in propelling you forward.
- You pay attention to proper breathing and relaxation as ways to increase your power, efficiency, and smoothness.

The main *difference* between ChiWalking and racewalking is noticeable.

- In ChiWalking it is not necessary for your front leg to be straightened. To the contrary, it is recommended that your leading leg be slightly bent and that you straighten it as it swings behind you. With racewalking, the legs are held straight throughout the ground-contact phase.

In essence, racewalking serves different needs for different racewalkers. Although for some people it was originally seen as a less injury-prone alternative to running (something that ChiRunning is also noted for), many racewalkers now seek the thrill and satisfaction of competitive challenges, pursue health and fitness goals, or simply enjoy the positive feelings that come with doing such a vigorous, total-body physical activity.

Racewalking may be a passion to be practiced and enjoyed whenever and wherever possible, or it may be a valuable form of exercise that helps keep the racewalker physically fit and emotionally balanced. For racewalkers, racewalking is one holistic form of fitness and athletic activity that is enjoyable yet challenging, liberating yet disciplined, and, above all, is accessible to do almost anywhere, anytime at almost no cost. Racewalking is a unique and powerful form of walking with broad appeal and a steadily growing level of participation. Racewalking is here to stay. (Author's note: Since the technique is best learned from an expert, I suggest you contact a local racewalking club or coach.)

THE CHIWALKING MATRIX

From the menu of walks presented in this chapter, I have devised a chart to make it easier to pick a walk appropriate to your needs. Along the top side of the chart is a list of all of the different walks presented in this book. In chapter 7, when you've created your program and you've decided how many walks per week you're going to do, just go to the chart and pick the walks for your program.

Down the left side of the chart there are four general categories of walks, each subdivided into the qualities and skills that they offer. An "X" in a box means that a particular quality matches up with a certain walk. You can read the ChiWalking Matrix from either direction. For example, if you want to get an aerobic walk into your schedule, you can go to the top and find "Aerobic Walk" and then follow that column down the chart to find out what you can expect to get from that particular type of walk.

On the other hand, if you know that one of your goals is to become a more relaxed person, you can go to the left side of the chart and find the column that says "Relaxing" or "Calming" or "Meditative," depending on what type of relaxation you're looking for. Then look at the top of the row to find out which walks offer what you're looking for. When you pick a walk, write it into your schedule. Sometime before that particular walk is scheduled to take place, be sure to go to the page that tells you exactly what to focus on during that walk.

These walks offer you a wide variety of choices. With a full menu of walks from which to choose, you'll always be able to create the type of energy you need to meet challenges that come up in your life. Use this chapter as a reference. Go to the ChiWalking Matrix and look through the list of qualities to find one that you're drawn to. When you find just the right one, you'll feel a resounding "yes!" come up from your body. When you can identify your needs, you're halfway to getting them met. Taking action and using one of the walks from the ChiWalking Menu will take you the rest of the way.

The ChiWalking Matrix ©2005

Category		Cardio Walk - pg. 103	Aerobic Walk - pg. 106	Hilly Walk - pg. 108	Loosening Walk - pg. 113	Upper-Body Walk - pg. 115	Chi-gathering Walk - pg. 116	Grounding Walk - pg. 123	Energizing Walk - pg. 125	Focusing Walk - pg. 126	Calming Walk - pg. 129	Walking Meditation - pg. 132	Racewalking - pg. 134
Physical	Strengthening	X	X	X		X							X
	Calorie Burning	X	X	X	X	X			X	X			X
	Loosening Joints	X	X	X	X	X					X		X
	Stretching	X	X		X	X							X
	Relaxing		X		X	X	X	X			X	X	
	Cardiovascular	X		X		X				X			X
	Aerobic	X	X	X	X	X			X	X			X
Mental	Focused Mind	X	X					X	X	X			X
	Spacious Mind		X				X				X		
	Relaxed Mind		X		X		X	X		X	X	X	
	Building Observer		X	X			X	X	X		X	X	
	Contemplative						X	X		X	X	X	
Emotional	Sensing Feelings		X				X				X	X	
	Calming				X			X		X	X	X	
	Heart Centered		X			X			X		X	X	
	Receptive		X			X	X	X			X	X	
	Energizing	X	X	X		X			X		X	X	X
	Expansive		X	X	X				X		X	X	
Metaphysical	Meditative							X		X			
	Directing Chi		X					X	X	X			X
	Big Picture		X				X				X	X	
	Building Presence		X				X	X		X	X	X	
Percentage MHR		70-80%	55-70%	60-75%	50-65%	65-70%	50-65%	50-65%	60-70%	60-70%	50-65%	50-65%	70-80%
Cadence (strides per minute)		70-80 spm	60-70 spm	60-70 spm	55-65 spm	65-70 spm	55-65 spm	55-65 spm	60-70 spm	60-70 spm	55-65 spm	55-65 spm	70-80 spm

For audio companions to these walks, please visit www.chiwalking.com.

CHAPTER SIX

Mindful Transitions

An early-morning walk is a blessing for the whole day.
—HENRY DAVID THOREAU

Everybody I know has some ritual they perform to transition into and out of sleep. My neighbor will absolutely *not* start his day until he's had his cup of coffee. My daughter will not go to sleep at night without a story, a cup of milk, and a few slices of apple to munch on. Unless I splash my face with water after getting out of bed, my day just doesn't start out right. It brings me into the moment and moves me into the day ahead. It's where I make the daily choice to be awake.

You could also say that transitions are a way of preparing yourself for what you are about to do. We all do it—all the time. From saying grace before a meal to anchoring our golf spikes into the green before making a putt, there are gestures we make, consciously or unconsciously, that prepare us for what we are *about* to do. This chapter will teach you how to mindfully transition *into* and *out of* your walks so that you can add true quality to your walk and bring the chi from your walk into the rest of your day. You'll learn how to approach each walk with physical preparation and mental intention and how to transition out of your walks with a relaxed body and a focused mind. If you do this, your ChiWalking practice will add more depth and a higher level of attentiveness to the rest of your life.

Along the way, you'll experience many "aha" moments and understandings about yourself, your body, and life in general. These new-found experiences and insights are fragile and need to be treated with utmost care. It's similar to having a child whom you need to "herd" constantly to get somewhere. Constant attention is needed so that she doesn't get away and get lost or separated from you. Likewise, the transitions in your day should have a sacred weight to them, for they are the glue that holds together what could otherwise become a disjointed set of activities with no common theme or direction. Consciously transitioning from one activity to another involves looking back, taking in, making a choice, and moving on.

TRANSITIONING INTO YOUR WALK

Before you go out for a walk there are two things you need to do: prepare your body and focus your mind. The key words here are *preparation* and *intention*. We'll take these two themes one at a time.

PREPARING YOUR MIND

The mental preparation for ChiWalking begins with assessing where you're at in the moment and where you're at in terms of the big picture, then deciding how best to accommodate the two if possible.

- Body Sense where you're at in the moment. Is there anything physically going on that you should consider while walking? Is there anything emotional or mental? If there are any adjustments to be made because of illness, stiffness, or any number of things, spend some time and think about what the adjustment will be. You might be tired and decide to do a much shorter walk than usual, or you might be feeling some soreness from skiing the day before. Whatever it is, be aware of it and ask yourself if there is anything going on that will affect your ability to have a great walk. You may then adjust your walk to take this into account.

- Look at the big picture. How does this walk fit in with your life as a whole? Will you be in nonstop business meetings for the next three days with no hope of getting away? How are you possibly going to walk in a three-day cancer walkathon in two weeks after having walked only two miles this month? Do you need to get your body looser for that tennis match tomorrow? What is going on in your life that could be positively affected by what you do in this particular session of ChiWalking? And how can you design your upcoming walk to accommodate that?

- Think about which focuses you'd like to practice on this particular walk. Are you having trouble leveling your pelvis? Maybe you should do the 1-minute-on, 1-minute-off exercise today. What would you like to get from this walk? How can you get the most from it?

- Make the decision to observe yourself during your ChiWalking. If you need to, set your beeper to go off every 3 minutes to remind you to check in with yourself to see how you're doing. You can't make improvements in your walking if you're not watching what's going on.

PREPARING YOUR BODY

Here's a tip to remember: the better you physically set up your body before going out to walk, the more enjoyable and fulfilling your entire walking program will be. If you set up the right conditions for a good walk, you'll likely have one. Or, if you feel any resistance to going out for a walk, moving forward in small preparatory increments makes getting out the door easier. Here are a few things to prepare your body for ChiWalking.

- Hydrate sufficiently. Be sure to drink plenty of water all day and especially before, during, and after walking. The movement of walking helps your body to eliminate toxins and water helps to flush that cellular waste out of your system. It is recommended that the average person consume ten 10-ounce glasses of water every day. That's a lot to keep up with and even more important to do if you're a regular walker. I carry a refillable plastic water bottle with me all day long. It holds 20 ounces and I try to drink four or five a day. The rule I go by is: if your pee is the same color as a taxicab, you're not drinking enough water.

- Fueling. Unless you're planning on walking for more than two or three hours, or you're diabetic and need to keep a close eye on your blood glucose levels, there's really no need to take food of any kind with you when you walk. I've never heard of anyone dying of starvation while walking, except for some guy who was trying to reach the South Pole. If you focus on food while you're walking, you're focusing on the wrong thing. Experiencing Nature in all its glory or working on your technique will keep your mind and your body plenty busy.

- Don't do vigorous walking right after eating. But taking a leisurely stroll to digest is a great idea, especially if you've just eaten a huge Thanksgiving dinner. Then it's good to get out and walk to counteract all of that tryptophan and to get as far away as possible from tempting thirds.

- Wear good shoes. I know this should be obvious, but you'd be surprised at how many people I see walking in shoes that either are too stiff or have elevated heels. Neither of these will do your feet or legs any good. Your shoes should be comfortable and should fit like bedroom slippers. Don't lace them too snugly or you risk irritating your arches.

- Do some prewalk body looseners. I do these religiously before every walk or run. They serve to relax your muscles and loosen your joints so that your walking will be more fluid. As I've mentioned previously, chi flows more readily through joints that are open and relaxed. So if you want your ChiWalking to do what it is meant to do, start each walk with a set of body looseners. I never stretch before I walk (find out why in the section on stretching).

These loosening exercises work to loosen and relax the main joint systems of the body. These are, in ascending order:

- ankles
- knees
- hips
- sacrum
- spine
- shoulders

Body Looseners

Begin by shaking out your whole body like you're a rag doll. Be sure to shake your arms and legs thoroughly.

Ankle Rolls

This will loosen all the ligaments and tendons in and around your ankles. Put your toe on the ground just behind your opposite foot. Keeping your toe on the ground, roll your ankle around in circles by using the circular rotation of your knee to create the motion. Do 10 clockwise circles and then 10 counterclockwise. Switch legs and repeat the exercise.

Knee Circles

This motion loosens the ligaments around your knees. Place your hands on your knees and move them around in clockwise circles, then reverse direction. Do 10 in each direction.

Figure 37—Ankle rolls: Balance your weight on one leg

Figure 38a—Knee circles: Bend at the hips, resting hands on the knees

Figure 38b—Swing your knees to the left

Figure 38c—Straighten your legs to the rear

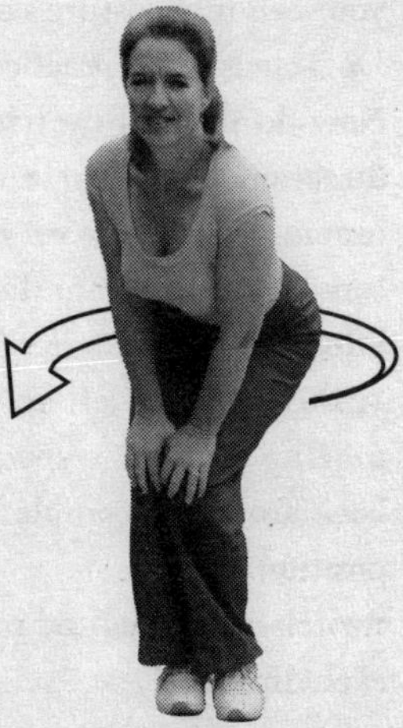

Figure 38d—Swing your knees to the right

Hip Circles

This exercise is easy but can be challenging for some people to learn. It is, however, one of the best exercises for loosening the ligaments and tendons in your hips and pelvic area in general. Just take it slowly and it'll come. I'll take you through it one step at a time.

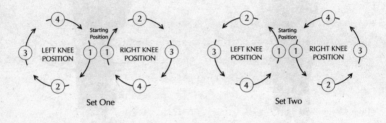

Set One   Set Two

1. Stand up straight with your best posture stance.
2. Relax your hips and move your right knee with a circular motion in a clockwise direction. Keep your whole foot in contact with the ground at all times. Do 5 "practice" circles and then return to your original posture stance.
3. Do 5 clockwise "practice" circles with your left knee.
4. Now do the full exercise with *both* legs moving in a clockwise direction but ½ cycle out of synch with each other. Start by moving your knees very slowly and it will come much easier. You can always speed up the motion as you get used to it. Start your knees going in circles by moving your right knee forward (to 12:00) and your left knee back (to 6:00). This will get them each moving in their respective clockwise circles. When they come back around to complete the circles, you will be in your starting position.
5. Switch directions and repeat the exercise. Start with 10 circles in each direction.

This exercise can be done anytime and anywhere, whether you're running or standing in line at the theater. It works to loosen your hips and pelvic area, which is where the bulk of movement happens in your running. Loosening this area makes your walking very fluid and easy.

Sacrum Circles

This exercise really works to loosen the area around your sacrum, which plays a key role in allowing you to have a loose and relaxed leg swing.

Place your hands on your hips, keep your back and spine in a vertical position, and tip your pelvis forward, to the side, to the back, to the opposite side, back to forward. Do 10 full circles with your pelvis and then change direction. When you get smooth at this one, it will feel like you're belly dancing. Keep your upper body as motionless as possible when you're moving your pelvis around in circles.

Figure 40a—Hip circles: Begin with your pelvis tilted up in front

Figure 40b—Tilt your pelvis to the left

Figure 40c—Tilt your pelvis down in front

Figure 40d—Tilt your pelvis to the right

Pelvic Rotations

Okay, you know where to start—get that posture really well aligned. Your feet are parallel and shoulder width apart. Level your pelvis. Don't use those glutes, and hold it level.

Next, put your left foot behind you about one shoe length—directly back so your feet are still shoulder width apart. *Keep your pelvis level.* That is one of the two main focuses of this exercise. Just keep going back to make sure your pelvis is level. You'll be amazed at how quickly it disengages when you're not thinking about it. Your weight is primarily on your forward (at this point right) foot, with some weight on the back foot.

Next, hold your arms at your sides with elbows bent at a 90-degree angle and your hands level with your waist.

With your pelvis level, *slowly* rotate your hips (the second main

Figure 41a—Pelvic rotations: Begin with your pelvis facing forward

Figure 41b—Rotate your pelvis to the left

Figure 41c—Rotate your pelvis back to forward

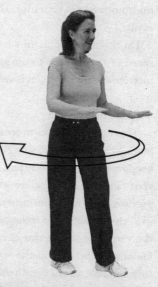

Figure 41d—Rotate your pelvis to the right

focus of the exercise). If you were looking straight down at your pelvis from a bird's-eye view, you would see your pelvis rotating clockwise, then counterclockwise; clockwise, then counterclockwise. Be sure to *not* rotate your upper body. You're holding your arms out at your sides to keep your shoulders facing forward while your hips are rotating (as they both should be when you're walking). Then take a step back and do the same exercise with your weight supported on the other leg. Do this exercise regularly, starting with 2 minutes on each leg and working up to 10.

You don't have to hold your arms out the whole time, but start the exercise this way until you get the feel of rotating your pelvis *without* rotating your shoulders. When you get a feel for this movement, you can bring your arms down and even put your fingers on the hip bones and encourage the movement.

The movement is actually originating at T-12/L-1, where your thoracic vertebra meets your lumbar vertebra. Your shoulders remain totally still, but the lower half of your body is rotating. If you're having a tough time with this, imagine the movement coming from your midspine and not your hips. That may help the movement come more easily.

Do this exercise as much as you can, eventually increasing the speed of the rotation to the speed of your cadence. You can use your metronome for this exercise as you do when you're walking.

Spine Rolls

This exercise works to loosen all the ligaments along your spine. Start by standing up straight and then bending over at the hips, keeping your upper-body posture straight. When you get as far over as your hamstrings will allow, stretch your spine in both directions by pushing back with your hips and craning your neck at the same time. (This will loosen your spine by creating micro-spaces between each of the vertebrae.) Hold this stretch for 5 seconds and then soften your knees and flop over at the waist and let your upper body just hang there, upside down. Bend your knees slightly, and starting with your tailbone, very slowly straighten yourself up one vertebra at a time until you are vertical again. Repeat 3 times.

Figure 42a—Spine roll: Begin in the standing position

Figure 42b—Bend at the hips and lengthen your spine

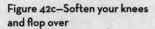

Figure 42c—Soften your knees and flop over

Figure 42d—Roll back up, starting at the lowest vertebra

Figure 42e—Rolling back up, keeping your chin down

Figure 42f—Rolling back up; chin comes up last

Figure 42g—Finish in the standing position

Spinal Twist

This one works to loosen the ligaments in your upper spine and shoulders, allowing you to have a relaxed arm swing. Stand with your feet together and your posture as upright as you can make it. Interlock your fingers behind your head with your elbows out to the sides. Keeping your hips in a stationary position, rotate your upper body to the right. As you twist your upper body around, drop your right elbow and raise your left elbow so that your upper body is bent over to the side. When you twist around, look down and try to see your opposite heel. Hold this position for a couple of seconds and then come back up to your starting position. Do the same thing to the left side. Repeat this exercise 3 times.

Figure 43a–Spinal twist: starting position

Figure 43b–Twist to the right, keeping hips facing forward

**Figure 43c—Tilt the upper body
and look for your opposite heel**

**Figure 43d—Come back up and
return to the starting position**

Shoulders and Upper Back

Begin by standing with your feet parallel and hip width apart, then step back with one of your feet so that the toe of your rear foot is lined up with the heel of the forward foot (as if you're starting a race) with your forward knee bent and your rear leg straight. Your weight should be a little more over the front foot than the rear one. Lean your upper body out over your forward leg, keeping your spine straight. Now let your neck, arms, and shoulders totally relax while you rotate your pelvis clockwise and then counterclockwise in a back-and-forth motion. Keep your arms and shoulders completely relaxed and let them be swung by the rotation of your pelvis. Feel the twisting motion in your lower back. Let your elbows *bend* as they swing behind your body so that the swinging motion doesn't pull on your shoulders. Now shake out your whole body and finish with the Grounding Stance.

Figure 44a—Shoulder looseners: Begin with feet staggered

Figure 44b—Swing your body to the right, keeping your arms and shoulders limp

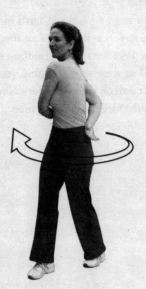

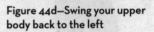

Figure 44c—Bend your elbow as your arm swings behind you

Figure 44d—Swing your upper body back to the left

Figure 44e—Bend your elbow as your arm swings behind you

Grounding Stance

In ChiWalking, every foot strike is an opportunity to feel your feet on the ground and your structure supported by the Earth. Do this exercise before every walk to get yourself grounded in your body and feel the power of the Earth beneath your feet.

Stand upright with your best posture. Place your feet hip width apart and parallel. Soften your knees and let your arms hang at your sides. Feel your posture being straight and tall. Put your attention onto your *dantien* (your center, located three fingers below your navel and 2 inches in, toward your spine.)

At the same time, drop your attention to the bottoms of your feet and press your big toes softly into the ground.

Now, connect your *dantien* to your feet with an imaginary line and let your feet support your *dantien*. This will have the effect of rooting you to the Earth. Hold this for 30 seconds. It will feel like a long time, but remember, it's worth every second if it leaves you feeling grounded. As I mentioned earlier, Master Xilin, my first T'ai Chi teacher, had me stand this way for the duration of our 90-minute class . . . for weeks! He would explain that it wouldn't do anyone any good to try to learn T'ai Chi if they couldn't feel grounded in their body first. Master Xu says that it's one of the most difficult stances in T'ai Chi to master. I'm still trying to get it.

The "Chi-Ball" Exercise

If you have access to one of those large stability balls, here's a great exercise to help get your body in the right alignment for the Grounding Stance.

1.   Start by holding the ball in front of your body with your arms wrapped around it. Soften your knees and let the weight of your body sink into your feet. Take a "body snapshot" of the position of your body and the physical sensation connected with it.
2.   Drop the ball while holding your body position.
3.   Relax your arms and let them fall to your sides without disturbing your body position. This is the Grounding Stance.

Once you've finished with your body looseners and your Grounding Stance, you're ready to go have fun. Feel the looseness in your body as you begin your walk.

Figure 45a—Grounding Stance, front view

Figure 45b—Side view: Notice shoulders, hips, and ankles are in alignment

STARTING YOUR WALK

Begin, as always, with aligning your posture before you take your first step. Once your column is aligned, just stand there and feel your feet under you and all of your chi-pipes straight and open. Review your intentions for the walk, start your countdown timer if you're using one, straighten up your column, level your pelvis—then simply fall forward and you're off! Be sure to start at a slow pace with a short stride to warm up. Your breathing should feel comfortable and not strained.

As soon as you begin to walk, the first thing to focus on is your posture. Feel your feet under you with each forward step. Every time your weight goes onto your foot, you should feel yourself in a one-legged posture stance. So as you start your walk, just think of it as doing a series of one-legged posture stances, one after the other. This is more easily felt if you keep your stride short. Keep your upper body centered over your feet and your lean engaged. Next, relax your pelvis and let it rotate with each stride. This will involve relaxing your lower back and sacral area. Every time your leg trails out to the back, let your hip go with it. This will get your pelvis swinging. When you're ChiWalking, you're always working to keep your core engaged and your column straight, while at the same time relaxing your hips, legs, shoulders, and arms. Remember the Needle in Cotton principle? That's what you're doing: staying solid inside and soft on the outside.

TRANSITIONING OUT OF YOUR WALK

I built custom furniture for fifteen years and one of my favorite things to do was clean up my shop at the end of the day. I'd take as much time as I needed to put away all of my tools and sweep up all the sawdust. My workday wouldn't feel complete unless I left the shop ready for the next day's work. Before I closed up each day, I'd take the time to look at what I had built and appreciate my efforts. I'd look back on the day's work and think about what I learned from my mistakes. I now do much the same thing at the end of my walks. I try to do what I can to help my body recover from the exertion and move smoothly into the next activity. I use my mind to assess how well the walk went, what I learned, and what I could do better.

When you're finished with your walk, it's great to allow your body and your mind to transition out of what you've just done. The key words here are *recovery* and *assessment.* Recovery is what you do with your body, and assessment is what you do with your mind. Remember, you're trying to establish a continuum here, so that you can carry some of what you gain from your walking into your next activity and your life in general. Let's start with how to recover your body.

The end of your walk is the time to ease off the gas pedal, to cool down, to appreciate yourself for what you just did, and to return your body to neutral before moving on to your next activity. Plan to stop your walk when you're still about 5 minutes from your destination. This will give you time to slow to a nice stroll and allow your heart rate and breathing to settle before moving on to your stretching. If you've just done an easy walk, you won't need much of a cooldown. But as your walks get longer and/or faster, you'll need to plan for more time to transition.

When you're finished walking, spend a couple of minutes strolling and relaxing your body on your way to wherever you're going to stretch. Take the time to do a *body scan* to appreciate how great it feels to have taken yourself out for a walk. Feel the chi energy moving through your body and what it feels like to be alive! Check in with your body to see if there is any tightness, soreness, or discomfort anywhere in your muscles or joints. Your body may be telling you that there's something in your technique that needs improvement. Try to isolate the specific body part that is speaking and make a mental note to watch it during your next walking session.

Take extra time during your postwalk stretching to focus on any areas of your body that feel particularly tight. If you're just beginning a walking program or upgrading an existing one, your muscles and joints might feel "well worked" (which is perfectly natural) but not necessarily sore. Always try to distinguish the difference. In the Troubleshooting section on page 166, we'll discuss how to correct some of the problems that may be causing pain and discomfort.

After cooling down from your walk it's *always* recommended to stretch before moving on to your next activity. A good stretching session will return your muscles to their neutral position. Here is a great series of stretches that will put the finishing touches on your workout.

STRETCHING

I never stretch before I walk because it is easy to pull a muscle when it's cold. Studies have shown that stretching before workouts does little if anything to improve the quality of the workout and can even create problems. Wasn't it Yogi Berra who said, "If you don't want to overdo something, don't do it in the first place?" If I have any tightness or soreness going into a walk, I do the looseners and then I just start off slower than usual and allow my body to gradually work its way into full movement.

Here are the basic stretches that will help you through a lifetime of walking. To ensure that all of your stretching is safe and not over-done, follow these simple rules:

- Stretch slowly and Body Sense how far to stretch each muscle group. Begin each stretch by doing it lightly, holding it for a few seconds, and then going more deeply into it as your body allows. Take at least 30 seconds for each stretch.
- Don't bounce when you stretch a muscle group; you could pull a muscle.
- Relax and breathe out as you initiate each stretch.
- Begin stretching within 10 minutes after ending your cooldown, while your muscles are still warm.
- If you've never done a stretch before, read the instruction very carefully and make sure you understand what to do. Then stretch lightly after your first few walks until you become more comfortable with the stretching positions and the sequence.

Calf Stretch

Stand about two shoe lengths away from a chair or wall and lean your body forward, keeping your heels on the ground. Move your pelvis toward the chair or wall, keeping your knees locked. This will stretch the calf muscles. Hold for a 10 count and repeat 3 times.

Figure 46—Calf stretch: Keep your heel down

Achilles Stretch

Same position as figure 46. Except that you are bending your knees as you lean into the chair or wall. Hold for a 10 count and repeat 3 times. An alternate way to do this stretch is to stand on a curb with your heels hanging off the edge. Stabilize yourself by holding on to a post. Lower your heels down one at a time by relaxing your ankles. Go only as far down as feels comfortable. Hold for 20 to 30 seconds.

**Figure 47—Achilles stretch: Bend your knee
and keep your heel down**

Hip Flexor and Upper Hamstring Stretch

Rest one foot on the top of something that is hip height and move your pelvis toward the heel that is raised. Hold for a 10 count and repeat 3 times on each leg. Keep your trunk vertical. For an even better hip flexor stretch, lock the elbow of the arm that is on the same side of your body as the foot that is on the ground and hold the arm straight up over your head as you press your pelvis toward your heel. When your hip flexor feels like it's at a maximum stretch, arch your

Figure 48a—Hip flexor stretch: Press your hips toward your heel

Figure 48b—Psoas stretch: hip flexor stretch with upper body twist

extended arm across your body and twist your upper body in the same direction. Hold for 30 seconds and repeat on the opposite side. This is one of the few stretches I've found that can actually stretch the psoas.

Hamstring Stretch

Place one heel on something that is hip height. Keeping both knees straight and your spine straight, bend at your hips and let your trunk fall toward your raised foot. Bend over only as far as your hamstrings allow. Hold for 20 seconds and repeat twice on each leg. You can also do this stretch sitting on the ground with your legs extended out in front of your body.

Figure 49—Hamstring stretch: Bend forward at the hips

Adductor Stretch

Sit on the ground with your knees straight and your legs spread as far apart as possible. Holding your back straight from your waist up, bend toward one leg for 20 seconds and then toward the other for 20 seconds.

Figure 50—Adductor stretch: Bend over forward from the hips

Quadriceps Stretch

With one foot on the ground, grab the ankle of your opposite leg and pull up on your heel. If you need to, you can stabilize yourself by holding on to a chair. Keep your knees together and pull your heel close to your butt. To stretch your quads even more, level your pelvis once you have your heel held up in place.

Figure 51—Quadriceps stretch: For a better stretch, hold knees together and pelvis level

Latissimus Dorsi (Lats) Stretch

This stretches the muscles of your back that are just below your shoulder blades and cover the outer ribs. Stand tall, with your feet spread a little more than hip width apart. Take one arm and reach over your head and grab that wrist with your opposite hand. Pull down on the crossed arm for 20 seconds and repeat on the other side.

Figure 52—Lats stretch: Pull down with your lower arm

Leg Drains

This is really one of my favorites. After your stretches, lie on your back with your feet propped up on a chair or wall (see figure 53). This does two things: it allows you to stop and rest, which is always nice, and it drains the old blood out of your legs, so that when you stand up again, you'll feel like you have a new set of legs under you. I do leg drains whenever I've spent a lot of time on my feet. This exercise has helped me so much over the years that I affectionately call it my

Figure 53—Leg drains (I've even napped in this position)

"miracle cure" for tired legs. Let yourself relax in this position for 3 to 5 minutes before getting up. While I'm lying there on my back, I often use the time to do my end-of-walk review.

Postwalk Assessment

Before going into your next activity, assess your walk, to see if there is anything you learned or would do differently next time. Here are some questions you might ask yourself:

- What were my intentions or focuses going into the walk?
- How did I do with remembering to do them?
- Did I feel them doing what they were supposed to do?
- Is there anything I learned during today's walk? Any realizations or understandings?

Keep a walking journal or log to record your progress. Many of us are not very good at acknowledging ourselves for the good things we accomplish. Keeping a journal is a great way to give yourself the gift of your efforts. Your walking will take on a more nourishing quality when you write down what you've done, because it's an opportunity to go back and replay the experience, which deepens your memory and understanding of each walk. This way, you'll be able to appreciate walking for much more than just a fitness program.

Before you start writing, take a moment to Body Sense your experience. Then write down those sensations. In this way, your walking journal will create a thread that connects all of your walks, weaving them together into a much larger picture, especially when you begin to notice the energetic difference of the various walks. Journaling will also help you to monitor and acknowledge positive changes in your walking and in your life. In chapter 7 you'll use your journal to record your vision, your goals, your plan, and your progress.

What to Do Between Walks: Practicing and Troubleshooting Your ChiWalking Form

Many people ask, "Can I practice the ChiWalking focuses when I'm not walking?" You bet. In fact, you can actually practice your ChiWalking focuses as much at other times as you can during your workouts. It's called *multitasking* and ChiWalking will make you a master of it. Here's a helpful hint to keep in mind: the more you practice the focuses *between* your ChiWalking sessions, the easier it will be to remember them *during* your sessions.

The following is a list of the most common walking-related problems and how to work with each. There are three possible modes you'll find your body in at any given point during your day: standing, sitting, and moving, so I've listed them according to the mode that best serves the issue.

Standing and Moving

The following are issues you can work with whenever you're standing or moving around. This means you can practice your ChiWalking focuses whenever you're on your feet, walking, doing sports, dancing, playing, waiting in line, standing at work, or going through an art museum. In this section, each topic will be followed by a brief description of the best ChiWalking focus to help the situation.

LOWER BACK PAIN

Most lower back pain is caused by compression of the lumbar vertebrae. To ease this compression and create more space between your discs, level your pelvis, which will strengthen your abdominal muscles and help to relax your lower back muscles. Hold your pelvis level (see page 74) as often as feels comfortable. Be sure to keep your knees slightly bent at the same time.

POOR POSTURE

I could work on this one every day for the rest of my life. Read the section about posture and practice the four steps starting on page 73 at least once a week until you memorize every step. Then practice the sequence as often as you can remember it. It helps me to "push against the sky" with the top of my head. I use the hourly beep on my watch to remind me to straighten up.

STRENGTHENING YOUR CORE

If your core is weak or if you would just like to have a stronger core, the best exercise is to level your pelvis whenever you're standing. You can also stand on one leg at a time for 1-minute to 5-minute intervals. The best way to do this one is to stand tall, soften your knees, and let all of your weight go onto one leg while resting the heel of your free foot on the ground in front of you.

WEAK ADDUCTORS

If your adductors are weak, you might tend to stand with your feet splayed out or spread apart.

Figure 54—Core-strengthening stance: a one-legged Grounding Stance

To strengthen weak adductors, stand with your feet hip width apart and parallel. To hold your feet parallel you should rotate your whole leg (at the hip joint) toward your centerline. If it is uncomfortable for you to have your feet parallel, rotate your legs only as far as feels acceptable and slowly increase the amount of inward rotation over a period of weeks or months as your adductors get stronger.

PRONATION

Whether you're standing or moving around, keep your feet parallel and feel the weight of your body pressing down on the outside edges of your feet. Lock this sensation into your memory so that every time you're on your feet, you're feeling it happen. Be sure to not lock your knees. Always keep them soft.

TIGHT CALVES

Whenever you're standing, you should try to sense the relative amount of pressure between your heels and the balls of your feet. Ideally, there should be equal pressure. If you have tight calves, chances are you notice more pressure under the balls of your feet. Work to constantly equalize and give your heels some of the work to do. Also, whenever you're standing around, shake out your lower legs one at a time by lifting them just off the ground and letting them hang limp while you shake your upper leg. When you're moving, you should never feel any tension in a calf muscle that is suspended above the ground.

LEVELING YOUR PELVIS

Whenever you practice leveling your pelvis, you should always straighten your upper body first (see page 74), then level your pelvis by lifting up your pubic bone with your lowest abdominal muscle, the pyramidalis muscle. It's a small, pyramid-shaped muscle that attaches to your pubic bone. Be sure to *not* use your glutes to level your pelvis, or your abdominals will never get any stronger. Who needs buns of steel anyway? Also, be sure *not* to use your upper abdominals to level your pelvis. You'll need to keep them relaxed so that you can belly breathe.

LOOSENING YOUR HIPS

Whenever you find yourself standing stationary in one place for longer than 5 minutes, you can do hip circles to loosen your hips. My T'ai Chi master would have me do them for half an hour at a time. They really work, even if you do only small circles. It's always better to focus on *more* circles rather than *bigger* circles. (See Body Looseners, page 142, for a complete description.)

RELAXING YOUR SHOULDERS

The shoulders are everybody's favorite place to hold tension. Here's a three-way method to get them to release tension:

1. Raise your shoulders and hold them tightly, doing scrunches either one at a time or both at once; hold the position for 5 seconds and then let them drop back down.

Figure 55a—Scrunch your shoulders

Figure 55b—Relax your shoulders

2. Next, internally pull down on your shoulders. Pretend you're holding a big bucket of water in each hand and pull your shoulders down with your arms. Pull down for 5 seconds, then relax them and let them return to their normal position.

3. Curl your shoulders forward for 5 seconds and then hold them back for 5 seconds.

Repeat these three steps as often as needed, or until you can feel blood beginning to flow to your brain again.

BODY SCAN

For practicing Body Sensing, this is the best tool there is. Do it as many times a day as you can remember to. I use the hourly beeper on my watch to remind me to do a body scan. I pretend I have an invisible MRI machine slowly scanning my body from head to toe for any tension, soreness, or joint tightness. It can take me anywhere from 1 second to 30 seconds to complete. If I come across any places that need some attention, I'll stop and do whatever is necessary before moving on. I do this one regularly throughout the day whether I'm standing, sitting, moving, or lying down.

SITTING

Although sitting is a nice way to rest your legs, it is unfortunately where many of us have developed poor postural habits from years of slumping in chairs, crossing our legs habitually, or continually adjusting our bottoms to accommodate spending hours on "end," either at our desks or in a car seat.

When I built furniture I rarely spent time sitting down. But in the past three years, since I began writing, I've had to sit at a desk for the first time in my adult life. I've had to learn to either keep my posture right or die an energetic death sometime in the midafternoon. If I'm sitting at my computer and I begin to lean back in my chair, my upper body collapses and my chi goes south, taking any available creativity with it. As I watch my energy slowly leak out of my body, I know that if I don't make a correction soon, I'll end up feeling like a deboned chicken.

Although sitting properly has always been work for me, I consider it to be *good* work, the kind I like to do. So I don't mind sitting up straight, because when I do, I can instantly feel more energy in my body. The following exercises can be done anytime you're sitting, whether you're eating a meal, working at your desk, meditating, driving a car, watching TV, attending a concert or a film, or sitting through a church service, a meeting, or a lecture. You'll never run out of opportunities to practice your ChiWalking focuses while sitting.

Here are some of the ChiWalking focuses along with some common problem areas that you can work on while you're sitting.

THE BODY SCAN

As I have mentioned before, you can never spend too much time Body Sensing. Do it often whenever you're sitting for extended periods and use it as a check-in tool to find out if your sitting is tiring or stressful to your body. Then use the following set of exercises and focuses to correct the situation and get yourself back on track.

BREATHING

If your job involves sitting and doing visually or manually detailed work, like drawing, designing, drafting, or assembly, you'll especially like this exercise because the more focused our minds and bodies are required to be, the less likely we are to breathe well. Hunching over your work constricts your lungs, reducing air intake, which restricts the amount of oxygen flowing to the brain. We end up at the end of the day with tense shoulders, stiff necks, and headaches, wondering how in the world it happened.

- Do you remember the second step of the posture exercise? It's the one where you put one hand on your belly button and the other just under your collarbone and straighten your upper spine by spreading your hands in opposite directions (see page 73). It's a simple move that you can repeat at regular intervals all day long. Again, use your watch beeper to remind yourself to do it regularly.

- It's also very important to belly breathe whenever you're sitting (see description on page 52). Sit with your pelvis level and on top of your "sitz bones." Find your sitz bones by putting your hands underneath your buttocks while sitting. The bones you feel are your sitz bones. Breathe through your nose if possible, slowly and deliberately.

- If you need a quiet mental break in your day, sit comfortably upright in your chair with your hands resting in your lap and your feet flat on the floor. Breathe slowly, taking about 5 seconds to inhale and another 5 seconds to exhale. Once you've set up a comfortable rhythm, spend the next 5 minutes doing *nothing* except watching your out-breath leave your body. You don't have to think about it or force it or *do* anything—just *watch*. This simple meditative exercise will clear your mind, settle your nerves, and center you. Now, how difficult is that to do? Try it and you'll see that it's one of the quickest and surest ways to get yourself into the present moment. When you emerge at the end of your 5 minutes, you'll feel physically rested and mentally sharp.

- If you need to get yourself out of some energy doldrums, you can do very short breaths in and out of your nose with your mouth closed. Do 20 short quick breaths followed by 1 big inhale, then repeat the cycle 2 or 3 times. It's an incredible energy booster and much better for you than another latte.

STRENGTHEN YOUR CORE

Anytime you sit in a chair, sit upright on the front and don't rely on the chair to support your back. Sitting up straight this way will build strong abs and hip flexors. Here are a couple more great ways to strengthen your core while sitting.

Do the Butt Walk

Sit on the floor with your legs together and extended straight out in front of you. Hold your upper body posture straight as an arrow. Cross your arms and place your hands on your opposite shoulders with your

elbows held at shoulder
height. Flex your ankles
so that your toes are
pointing straight up into
the air. Now, walk for-
ward on your sitz bones
by rotating your pelvis,
taking 10 "steps" on each
side while sliding your
legs forward (without
lifting your legs *at all*).
When you've done 10 for-
ward, do 10 back. If you
do this exercise once
every day, you'll have
great abs, a very healthy
psoas, and a strong set of
internal obliques. You
can't do much better than
that from a single exer-
cise.

Figure 56a—Right leg "walks" forward

Use a Stability Ball

I had lower back pain
for many years, so learn-
ing how to sit in a chair
for extended periods
without hurting myself
has been a special chal-
lenge. One thing that
helped me immensely
was using a stability ball
for my desk chair. That's
right. I still work at my
desk while sitting on a
large stability ball. I have

Figure 56b—Left leg "walks" forward

seen a set of casters that will hold the ball so that you can scoot around the floor at your desk without having to roll the ball. Sitting on one of these balls for extended periods not only strengthens the muscles along your axis, but it will also keep them moving and flexing instead of rigid, as typically happens in a regular chair.

I can do pelvic circles while keeping my upper body motionless and come away feeling my sacrum and lower back relaxed but strong. I like it because I can keep my pelvis mobile while I'm sitting, which is difficult to do in a regular chair. I can do pelvic circles all day long if I feel like it. It keeps my sacrum and hips flexible and there is no stiffness when I stand up. I highly recommend this one.

So what if everyone in your office makes fun of you? It's a perfect opportunity to practice Nonidentification (see page 181).

Use Your Chair Wisely
- When you're sitting in a chair, sit only on the front half of the chair seat (with your tailbone approximately over the support post of the chair) and don't use the chair back to support your upper body. If this is new to you, begin by doing it once an hour for 5 minutes and then increase the amount of time over a period of weeks. This will strengthen your abdominal muscles for your walking practice.

  If you're experiencing any low back pain while walking, be sure to consult with your doctor before doing any of these exercises.
- **Relax your shoulders.** This might sound radical or even Victorian, but I think the worst thing ever added to chairs was armrests. Most of them are too high, which means that if you're resting your elbows on them, you're actually supporting some of your upper body weight with your shoulders, which were not designed to support your body. Whenever I'm sitting in an airplane I notice that I can feel tension in my upper back and neck when my arms are on the armrests—and it goes away when they're not. Try it and you'll see.

  Whenever you're sitting in a chair at your desk, once every hour, drop your arms at your sides, shake them out, and then let them just dangle there for 30 seconds. Then do a couple of shoulder rolls on each side and continue on with your work. If you practice this regularly and hourly during your day, I can guarantee you'll carry less tension in your shoulders and you'll be able to keep them relaxed while you're walking.

- **Loosen your hips.** Whenever you're "chair-bound" for more than an hour, it's always a good idea to stand up and do 30 hip circles in each direction once every hour. This keeps your joints loose all day and can even help relieve sciatica.

- **Feel the twist of your spine.** Here's a way to use your desk chair to help relax your lower back. This requires a chair that swivels. Sit upright with your tailbone directly over the axle on which the chair swivels. Pull your chair up to the desk so that your elbows can comfortably rest on the desktop. Hold your feet off the ground (raise your chair if you need to). Now swivel your chair back and forth keeping your elbows on the desk and your shoulders and upper body motionless while leveling your pelvis and allowing your lower body to rotate back and forth with the chair. This loosens your lower back by creating a slight twist along your spine from the midpoint on down.

In ChiWalking, your pelvis should rotate to the right (clockwise) as your right leg swings behind you. This allows your hip to follow your leg swing. A twist in the opposite direction happens with the motion of your left leg. The bottom line of this exercise is simply to feel the twisting of your spine, so that you'll know how it should feel when you're walking.

Practicing the ChiWalking focuses between your workouts will help you to master the ChiWalking technique relatively quickly *and* it will add a new level of consciousness to your waking life by keeping you aligned, engaged, balanced, attentive, and most of all moving forward healthfully.

TRANSITION INTO YOUR DAY

It's Monday morning and Katherine and I are just sitting down to write together after doing our Monday routine. Katherine gets Monday mornings to herself and I take care of Journey and get her off to school. Here's what Katherine does. She begins by washing her face and doing her morning meditation. Then she's off to go walking and then swimming, which has been her routine for years. Believe me, the week doesn't go well for any of us if Katherine doesn't get her Monday mornings.

I begin Mondays as early as possible to get my morning program done before Journey wakes up. When she does wake up, my focus is on creating a nice, settling but fun morning routine for her. She wakes up ready to play, so we give her playtime before she gets dressed and sits down to breakfast. She's happier at school and has a better day when she starts her day with some playtime with one of us. These routines are how we transition into the week and into the day. We rely on these transitions to add quality to our family life. Otherwise, we are so busy that our lives can turn to chaos in an instant. In the long run the transitions are as valuable as any of the activities we do, and maybe even more so.

It's been said that life is "one damn thing after another," and sometimes it may seem that way. Transitioning mindfully adds continuity and depth to your experience so that your day adds up to more than just "one damn thing after another." Your walking program becomes not just another thing on your to-do list, but an activity that has added dimension, value, and quality to your life. For some of us, that can be the glue that holds it all together.

CHAPTER SEVEN

Creating Your ChiWalking Program

"Would you tell me, please, which way I ought to go from here?"
"That depends a good deal on where you want to get to," said the Cat.
"I don't much care where—" said Alice.
"Then it doesn't matter which way you go," said the Cat.
"—so long as I get *somewhere*," Alice added as an explanation.
"Oh, you're sure to do that," said the Cat, "if you only walk long enough."
—LEWIS CARROLL, *ALICE'S ADVENTURES IN WONDERLAND*

E very time I cross the Golden Gate Bridge, I think of the vision-
aries who conceived it and followed it through to completion
and how they had to make all the right choices along the way in
order for that bridge to be a functional piece of artwork that would be
appreciated around the world for generations. It is a monument to
great vision, impeccable planning, and the human capacity to accomplish great things.

The two major themes of program development are having a
vision for yourself and consistently making the choices that move you

in that direction, the same components that went into manifesting the Golden Gate Bridge in its full glory. Anything that is of value requires the same approach.

Lifelong health and fitness happen when you make mindful, positive choices over an extended period of time—or for the rest of your life. Whenever you do something consistently for a long time, it works on you in a deep, powerful way. For example, let's say you decide to never say the word *love* in conversation for a year. Every time the urge to use the word *love* would come up, you would have to use other words that would more clearly and specifically explain how you feel. This exercise would force you to dig deeper for the best words to explain your feelings, rather than rely on the beautiful but nonetheless vague catchall word *love*. Choosing to do this would make you more aware of your feelings because you would have to voice them more precisely. If you did this consistently for a year, I guarantee you would be a different person at the end of that year. It's a challenge to do it just for a day!

When you have a well-thought-out walking program and stay consistent with it, it can help you in ways you might not even imagine. Granted, walking will get your *body* into great condition. But in order to stay on the track of lifelong health, you must exercise your *mind* as well. Mindfulness is a lifelong practice for exercising your mind to work in a positive and productive way. For most of us, our mind is our worst liability. It is unharnessed and wild. It gets distracted easily and attaches itself to anything even remotely attractive. So why not give your mind something good to feed on instead of the often-negative wanderings that it usually engages in?

TRUST YOUR BODY'S KNOWLEDGE

The only surefire way to stay with a program is to find a program that has a purpose that you can *feel in your body*. Anything else is just a mind game, which is hit or miss, at best. There is not a more convincing argument than an experience you've had in your body. *That's* what will motivate you. What did it *feel* like when you weighed twenty pounds less? How good did it feel when you used to walk every day? How energetic were you when you ate better and exercised regularly? How did you get into great condition before? All of those positive experiences are forever locked in your body's memory and are there to draw upon when you need them for inspiration. Your mind can play games with you and rationalize why you should exercise, but your body will give you very clear and undeniable reasons. You can't argue with the body because it doesn't lie.

STAY HEALTHY FOR THE REST OF YOUR LIFE

To help build a picture around the concept of lifelong health, I need to bring in an authority on the subject, my old friend, the *I Ching*. It is the ancient, quintessential book of Chinese wisdom—studied and annotated by such luminaries as Confucius and Lao Tse, and perennially the most valuable book in my library. There is a chapter entitled "Duration" in which the *I Ching* gives a definition for *duration* that Webster could only aspire to. I use this definition of duration to describe the quality that every program should have. Read it a couple of times, then take a minute to think about what it is saying.

> **Duration:** ". . . the self-contained and therefore self-renewing movement of an organized, firmly integrated whole, taking place in accordance with immutable laws and beginning anew at every ending."

It then continues with this gem:

> "Whatever *endures* can be created only gradually by long-continued work and careful reflection."

This definition left by ancient Chinese philosophers was meant to give us the ideal prescription for how to develop a successful lifelong practice. The two adjectives from the definition that spark my thoughts are *organized* and *firmly integrated*.

Organized implies that all of the elements of your program should be well planned and well placed. By *well planned*, I mean that your walking program should be built around your vision of what you want to accomplish by exercising, taking into account injury prevention and gradual buildup. *Well placed* means that whatever program you come up with contributes to the balance of the rest of your life.

Firmly integrated implies that your program needs to become as much a part of your life as eating, brushing your teeth, and anything else you wouldn't think of skipping—anything that you do simply because of who you are. You don't force it into your life, but over time it becomes a part of you. When you're first starting a walking program, there is a tendency to identify yourself as a "walker." It's like being in a club and seeing yourself as part of a larger group. But the idea of duration is to get to the place where walking eventually becomes such a regular part of your life that you no longer define yourself as a walker—walking is just a part of your everyday existence and a reflection of your life practice.

When we speak of having a program that provides lifelong health, we're talking about introducing a mindful, systematic program that does the following:

- creates physical and mental balance in your life
- moves energy through your body on a regular basis so that your muscles and organs stay vibrant
- teaches you how to relax, so that your life takes on a new level of ease
- teaches you how to focus, so that your mind will last longer
- teaches you how to breathe well, so that your muscles and organs are never starved of oxygen
- builds in you a sense of self-confidence and trust in your body
- ensures that healthy movement is a regular part of your life's activities
- helps your posture to stay aligned as you age

No matter how old you are, if you want to continue having energy in your body well into your elder years, the best time to start the process is *now*. The old saying "Use it or lose it" definitely applies to our bodies. If you want to build lifelong energy, you must be consistent with your exercise program, almost rhythmic in its execution. In all of my experience with training groups and individuals, I've found that the best way to be consistent is to make the choice to be so—and that ball *never* leaves your court.

THE PRINCIPLE OF NONIDENTIFICATION

The Principle of Nonidentification, inherent in T'ai Chi and Chi-Walking, is crucial for creating a program. Nonidentification is when you can take your personal *preferences* out of the planning process and replace them with your real *needs*. This will help you to develop a program that is effective in creating change in your life. The Rolling Stones put it very well in their song "You Can't Always Get What You Want." That song came out over thirty-five years ago and holds just as true today.

When it comes to your health and fitness, be guided less by what you want and more by what you need. What you *want* might be unrealistic, idealistic, or even possibly harmful. But what you *need* is just that: a legitimate need around which you can build a plan. If you have a history of heart disease in your family, you *need* to do whatever it takes to break that legacy, or you could be checking out early. That means you need to watch your diet, you need to exercise your heart, and you need to be vigilant in order to escape your genetic heritage.

You might *want* to exercise only 15 minutes a day, but given your caloric intake, you might *need* to walk for 45 minutes a day (or lower your caloric intake) to keep from gaining weight. You might *want* to get out and hike trails with a pack on your back, but you might *need* to get in shape first because you're starting from scratch with an exercise program. You might *want* to walk in a 3-day walkathon for breast cancer, but you might *need* to build up slowly so that you don't end up injured and sidelined when the big event rolls around. Separating your wants from your needs is a big job but well worth the effort if you want to have a successful program and reach your goals. When it comes to practicing Nonidentification, you have to do what your body tells you is best for you—not what your mind *thinks* is best for you.

Nonidentification begins with doing a personal assessment so that you can accurately determine your best starting point—realizing that there is *always* a gap between where you are and where you want to be.

Keep a Journal

Keeping a personal health journal will help you add an enduring quality to your walking program. In order to create the best program for yourself *and* keep track of all your progressive steps, you will need to record your vision, your weekly program, and the results of your good efforts. The process of writing will reinforce your commitment. You can keep an ongoing record of your walks, your understandings, realizations, insights, body sensations, and lessons, not to mention your mileage, weight loss, resting heart rate, and whatever other pieces of personal data you choose to collect.

In this chapter we'll return again to the Five Mindful Steps and use them to design a walking program tailored to fit your needs. Here's an overview:

The Five Steps for Designing a ChiWalking Program
1. Get Aligned with Your Vision
   - Write down your vision of what you want for yourself in terms of an exercise program.
   - Get aligned with your starting point today—with your present. Do a personal assessment of your physical state and mental attitude to find square one.
2. Engage Your Core by Creating Goals
   - Write about what you *really need to do* to work toward your vision. Create intermediate, specific goals with shorter time frames of up to one year.
3. Create Balance in Your Weekly Program
   - Balance your weekly program relative to your real, legitimate needs. Balance your program in a way that works in your everyday life.
4. Make a Choice from the ChiWalking Matrix
   - Choose which types of walks are best for moving you in the

direction you'd like to go with your fitness program and to nourish and balance you energetically.

5. Move Forward with Smart Program Upgrades
   • Move forward by leaning into your program, and keep your momentum with smart program upgrades.

1. Get Aligned with Your Vision

Your vision is the fuel that will energize your walking program. Writing down a personal vision is important for laying the groundwork for anything you want to accomplish in your life. Having a well-written, vivid vision is like having the future pull you forward into itself. All good things start with the imaginings in our minds. Even a well-planned meal first starts with someone planning that meal. If Sunday dinner gets that much planning and forethought, don't your health and well-being deserve as much? Your vision is what you will focus on to carry you through the rough spots and roadblocks that may threaten your program.

Make your vision for your health and energy broad, expansive, and energetic. Write this vision in your journal. You can work on clarifying it or expanding it over time, but the first time you write it can often be the most telling. Give yourself an undisturbed half hour and write down how you would like to see yourself in terms of your health and energy in ten years, then in five years, then in one year from now. How would you like to feel day to day? How would you like to feel when you wake up in the morning and go to sleep at night?

Now *imagine* reaching those goals—really take the time to stop and imagine being at the health and fitness level you would like. Write down how it would *feel* physically and emotionally to live at that level of health and fitness. Be as specific as possible about all the benefits of looking and feeling great. This step is to help you get aligned with your best vision for yourself. It is important to have a clear vision so that you can go back to it whenever you encounter difficulties in your training.

GET ALIGNED WITH WHERE YOU'RE AT TODAY

It might sound obvious and simplistic, but the best way to begin any program is to start from where you are. And if you have good information about your current state, you can then easily track your progress. You'll start by doing a physical assessment of your current health and energy level and then an assessment of your mental attitude.

Start by writing a very accurate and honest personal assessment for yourself so that there is no mistake about what you are capable of doing in the beginning stages of your program. The problem that a lot of people have is knowing where they're really at. With that in mind, here are some suggestions of what to consider when determining your own square one. Be deeply honest with your answers. No one else has to see your journal or your answers.

What to include in your assessment:

- the basics: age, weight, and a general impression of your health and energy level
- how much exercise and what kind of exercise you currently get
- how you feel after this exercise
- the positive aspects of your health and energy
- time of day you have the most energy and feel your best
- time of day when your energy is at its lowest point
- any health issues and concerns that you have

ARE THERE ANY RED FLAGS?

Do you have any current mitigating health-related factors that you should consider as you move into a regular exercise program? Are you on any medications or do you have any conditions that may be affected by physical activity (e.g., high blood pressure, stroke, heart disease, injury, diabetes, recent surgery)? Please make sure you get a thorough physical and that you address any major health issues with your physician.

BENCHMARKS FOR PROGRESS

Here are two simple self-tests for you to measure your starting point and to track improvements in your fitness level. These are not a measure of your fitness level but are a relative measure for you to track your progress over time.

1. Determine Your Resting Heart Rate

First of all, as a baseline reference point, it is important to know your resting heart rate (RHR). As your level of conditioning improves, you will notice a drop in this number, so it's good to look at it occasionally so that you can chart your progress toward better health. This will provide plenty of reassurance when doubts arise about the effectiveness of your program.

To find your resting heart rate: Lay your watch within easy reach from where you're sleeping before you go to bed. When you wake up in the morning, before you do anything else, reach for your watch and take your pulse by holding your thumb on your neck just next to your throat while holding your watch in the other hand so that you can read it. Count the number of heartbeats in 15 seconds and then multiply that number by 4 to get your beats per minute. Then jump out of bed and rush over to your log and enter the number before you forget it. Then slowly return to your bed and get back under the covers, knowing that you did your good deed for the day. Do this once a month or track it as often as you wish. Those of you who are starting off in the lower end of the fitness spectrum will get to enjoy the largest drop in this number, so you have a lot to look forward to.

2. Do the 20-Minute Walking Test

Another good way to measure your progress is to begin by doing a 20-minute walking test. Put on comfortable walking clothes and shoes and find a place to walk where you can return for future walking tests. A local track works best, but a specific route in your neighborhood will also work. Be sure that you're walking on a flat surface: hills can skew your results. Check your watch and walk for 20 minutes at a fast pace. You should be able to talk, but not comfortably. At the end of your 20 minutes, do two things: (1) take your pulse immediately, and (2) measure how far you have walked. When you return home, enter both numbers into your journal or log. If you do your walk along a bike path or through your neighborhood, simply write down what landmark you were next to at the end of 20 minutes.

If you repeat this 20-minute walking test on the same course every month, you will notice that you will either (1) cover more distance in the same 20 minutes, or (2) finish with a lower heart rate. This is a very personally rewarding way to check in on your progress.

ATTITUDE ASSESSMENT

Once you have written down all the physical aspects regarding your health and energy, do the same for the mental processes that are so integral to a fitness program. Note the positive aspects of your mental attitude, such as the voices in your head that encourage you to keep up your fitness program. If you have strong willpower and are consistent with your fitness program, write *that* down as an asset. Then write down areas where you struggle. Take a good look at the mental voices that have pulled you off track in the past. Write down some of these one-liners that your mind will use to pull you off your fitness program. Think ahead and prepare so you will be able to override these voices before they even start talking. Get to know these voices for what they are and know when they typically come up. Get a jump on these negative voices, because once they start talking they're hard to shut up.

Here are some of the one-liners you might hear:

"Walking isn't that important, so missing a walk isn't going to make a big difference."

"I'm too busy and I have more important things to do than take a walk."

"I walked yesterday. I can skip a day."

"I'm too tired."

"I just ate and just want to watch my favorite show."

Get the picture?

By getting aligned with your vision and with your current physical and mental attitude, you're ready to *engage your core* and pinpoint your goals and strategies.

2. Engage Your Core by Creating Goals

Now it's time to "engage your core" and create the steps that will take you from your current state to your vision—your personal goals. When you engage your core, you move forward from a place deep within yourself and from your deepest source of power. You want to choose reasonable, enticing short-term goals that have meaning and value for you. These goals should move you toward your vision.

A goal can be anything that you want to accomplish through your walking program, from weight loss to distance, from increasing self-confidence to lowering your blood pressure. At least some of your goals should be *specific* and *measurable* and capable of being accomplished within a time frame of three months to a year. If you have a goal that spans more than one year, you might think of breaking it up into two smaller and more manageable parts. If you have a history of not being able to make your goals, it is best to choose a goal that can be accomplished in a relatively short time frame. When in doubt, always go back to the principle of Gradual Progress and start *small* with your goals. Weekly or monthly goals are also a good idea. Save the big goals for when your skill level and personal momentum can better match the size of the project.

What are your goals and aspirations in the physical, emotional, mental, and metaphysical areas of your life? Here are some ideas to get you started:

Physical Goals
- A stronger body
- A healthy heart
- Weight loss
- Complete a 5k, 10k, or marathon walking event
- Cross-training for another sport
- Walk a given distance or speed
- Keep up with your kids or your dog
- Recover from surgery or an injury
- Improve Body Sensing skills

- Gain more freedom of movement
- More energy

Emotional Goals

- Greater self-esteem
- More social interaction
- Deeper relationship with Nature
- Emotional balance
- Time to sort out life's challenges and problems
- Lower anxiety

Mental Goals

- Better mental focus
- Better (positive) use of your mind
- Mental challenge
- Expanding your mind, being open to new ideas
- Better organizational capacity
- Better body-mind connection

Metaphysical Goals

What are your metaphysical goals and how can a ChiWalking program help you move toward those goals? The term *metaphysical* is used here to include anything in your life that has an inwardly energetic and invisible quality, such as:

- Having a sense of centeredness
- Having the ability to be Nonidentified
- Understanding Natural laws
- Experiencing a sense of wholeness in your life
- Being in the present
- Appreciating the gift of life

Don't feel obligated to come up with goals within all of these categories. The best way to begin a program is to start with where you're at now. If you don't feel drawn to setting metaphysical or emotional goals now, don't worry. You can always come back and do them when the urge (or the need) comes up. Goals should always come from your core, your center, from inside of you, not from other people's ideas of what you should be doing. I keep an ongoing list of goals that I'm either working on now or thinking of working on sometime in the future.

For right now, choose the goal or goals that you want to work toward. Write them down and write down how you will know when you have accomplished each—what is the time frame and the specific, measurable outcome you hope to see? In your journal, keep a whole page for each goal so you can track your progress on that one page.

3. CREATE BALANCE IN YOUR WEEKLY PROGRAM

It's now time to put your personal assessment and goals together to create a good workable walking schedule that will be perpetually moving you toward your goals, year in and year out. A tightrope walker can walk only as far as she can remain in balance. Likewise, you'll find it easier to carry on a regular walking program if it is in balance with the rest of your life and in balance with your physical and energetic needs.

In our society, we talk a lot about how important it is to stay physically fit and healthy, but the amount of time we devote to physical fitness is relatively small. In order to meet your real needs, you must prioritize being physically active and make your fitness program as successful and easy to stay with as possible. Working to rewire your nervous system and change how your body moves can be challenging, but your program itself shouldn't be a struggle. The struggles you meet during your workouts are *good* struggles and necessary ingredients for growth. The best way to create an integrated, healthy walking program that will last for years is to make a place for it to exist alongside everything else you love and need to do. Only then can you call it *balanced.*

Before we get started, let's review some of the health benefits of walking. According to most studies that I've found, in order to get the most health benefits from walking, you want to build up to a program of walking at least 6 days a week (preferably 7) for 30 minutes a day (or less for those 65 and older). This works out to about 3 hours or more of walking per week. In case you need some encouragement, here are a few reminders of what benefits lie in store.

- For people between 50 and 79, 2½ hours per week of brisk walking cut the risk of heart attack and stroke by about one third.
- A brisk 30-minute walk, just 3 times a week, was just as effective as antidepressant medication in relieving the symptoms of major depression in middle-aged and elderly people.
- Two and a half hours or more of walking per week, in combination with a healthier diet, did more to ward off diabetes than did the popular diabetes-prevention drug Metformin.
- For men ages 40 to 84, daily moderate exercise cut the risk for colon cancer and polyps in half.
- Women ages 70 to 87 who walked 3 days a week for 10 weeks significantly increased HDL (good cholesterol) while decreasing triglyceride levels. Other studies show that moderate exercise decreases LDL (bad cholesterol).
- Older adults who walk the most have a lower risk of dementia and age-related intellectual decline.

Many of these studies show that as you increase the time spent walking, the benefits are even greater. With all of this in mind, here are some guidelines to help you define your walking program. Be *as specific as possible*—it's really important that you pin yourself down here.

- If you're a beginner, you can start with 3 to 5 days per week, depending on your fitness level. As your level of conditioning improves (and it will!), 30 minutes or more per day, 6 or 7 days a week is recommended for an effective fitness program. Write down **how many days per week** you plan to walk.
- Write down **which days of the week** are the best days for you to walk.
- For *each* of those days, write down what would be the optimal **time**

of day for you to walk. Many people find that it's easier to do their walks in the morning, before the distractions of the day begin to pour in.

• Write down **how many minutes** you plan to walk on each of the days you have scheduled. Be sure to factor in any travel time or transition time so that you have a good gauge of how much time your total workout will take.

• Write down **the days and time blocks** of all of your weekly walks. Treat these blocks of time like precious appointments so that you can have a polite way of refusing someone's request for your time. Better yet, invite them along!

By creating a walking program that can be realistically incorporated into the rest of your life, you are more likely to walk regularly. Treating your exercise program in this way will help you to give it the importance it deserves.

4. MAKE A CHOICE FROM THE CHIWALKING MATRIX

After you have completed your self-assessment and determined your weekly walking days and times, you can use the ChiWalking Matrix to pick and choose the specific walks you'd like to insert into your schedule. This is where you get to create your own personally tailored program. There are two things to keep in mind when choosing walks for your program: working on your ChiWalking technique and improving your conditioning level. The benefit you derive from your program depends on the quality of your effort, so begin *every* walk by practicing your walking technique.

In the early stages of your program pick walks from the "Physical" category of the Matrix as they will help you improve your technique and your conditioning. ChiWalking is a fitness program, because physical fortitude is the foundation for your mental and emotional health. The scientific studies mentioned above demonstrate that your emotional and mental well-being are highly influenced by physical fitness and activity.

With a good technique, all of the walks in your program will provide you with more chi because your body will be aligned, relaxed, and moving as it should. Since good form is the foundation of all that comes after, it is important to constantly work to improve it. In this way, it is just like a yoga practice where one is always working to improve one's skills in each posture. Chi energy will move through your body whenever you set up the right conditions for energy to flow, and it's all based on good technique.

5. MOVE FORWARD WITH SMART PROGRAM UPGRADES

The first four steps of the Five-Step Process are like preparing for a vacation. You've chosen your destination, you've made all the travel plans, you've chosen what to bring, you've packed, and now all you have to do is grab your bags and step out the door. If you've been thorough with the first steps, Moving Forward is like the gentle lean in the ChiWalking technique.

This last step is not just about the first few weeks of your program, but about keeping momentum for a lifetime of health and energy. You do this through keeping your program energetic and Moving Forward with program upgrades.

If your vision is to be an inspiration to your grandchildren with your vitality and energy, and you have a one-year goal to walk a half marathon to raise money for your favorite charity, and your current longest walk is 30 minutes, your weekly program is going to need regular upgrades to help you reach your goal.

Here's a formula to help you safely and effectively increase your fitness and endurance level:

- You can increase your walking time each week up to 10 percent.
- You can upgrade two walks each week (not more). Upgrades include:
  - more time or distance
  - adding hills or more difficult terrain
  - increase in speed and/or cadence
  - increase in number of walks per week

Caution: Program upgrades need to be relative to what your body can handle, so Body Sense and always ask your body if an upgrade is appropriate. Maybe walking half a marathon is possible in one year's time, but don't try to start from scratch and walk 13.1 miles in 3 to 6 months unless you have the necessary physical conditioning to support it.

When you overdo, you will *lose* momentum by incurring injury or pain, or getting overfatigued. Moving Forward is about the long haul. It is about creating a program that endures for a lifetime and becomes an expression of how you live. This process gets impeded when you push too hard too soon or set unreasonable goals.

To Move Forward toward lifelong health and energy and your personal vision, create a regular rhythm with your walking program, so, like the seasons, it is reasonably predictable but always changing appropriately with the time.

Remember the quote from the *I Ching* that I used in the beginning of the chapter: "Whatever *endures* can be created only gradually by long-continued work and careful reflection." Your program can be as rich as you want to make it. The choice is yours—for now or for a lifetime.

CHAPTER EIGHT

Hiking: Welcome to Off-road Walking

There is nothing like walking to get the feel of a country. A fine landscape is like a piece of music; it must be taken at the right tempo. Even a bicycle goes too fast.
—PAUL SCOTT MOWRER, *THE HOUSE OF EUROPE*

I recently went for a hike up our local mountain. It's about 2,500 feet in elevation gain and about 6 miles of trail, bottom to top. As I left the trailhead I was freezing. The day was overcast as winter blanketed everything with a bone-rattling chill. Starting out, I thought to myself that I really didn't want to spend a day hiking in the dampness, but that sooner or later I'd warm up from hiking and the lack of sunshine would be more tolerable. So I trudged on.

About 45 minutes later, after gaining about 1,000 feet in elevation, I spotted a small hole in the clouds and my heart lifted. Then, as I climbed higher, the clouds began to get wispier with a distinct blue peeking through. Soon I found myself in full blazing sunshine, looking across the tops of the clouds from which I had just emerged. From my new vantage point there was not a cloud in the sky. It was a brilliant day. Below me was an ocean of clouds enveloping the valleys with little hilltop islands poking up every now and then. It was definitely a *National Geographic* moment. I spent the next half hour scrambling up to the summit and after spending a few quiet moments to take in the spectacular view and feel the energy moving through my body from my workout, I began my descent back to the world below. Sure enough, about halfway down the mountain I reentered the cloud zone and was once again freezing until I got back to my car.

Looking back on my hike, I reaffirmed once again why I love hiking so much. I have read in more than a few places that the definition of hiking is "leaving the pavement behind." As soon as you step off the road or the sidewalk and onto dirt, you can instantly feel the texture of Nature beneath your feet. It's not all flat or smooth or straight. The joy of hiking is in *not* knowing what you're going to come up against when you're strolling through Nature. You could be walking across a dry riverbed in the morning and wading in ankle-deep water across the same spot in the afternoon. I've had hikes in the Colorado Rockies where I experienced all four seasons in a single afternoon. So after many hours of sitting at my computer, I go hiking to refresh my soul, and doing so opens up my heart again in no time flat.

I also like to think of hiking as *fitness with a view.* It's a feast for your heart and your eyes. Walking in Nature challenges your reflexes, leaves you clearheaded, and develops your ability to surrender and adapt to something much larger than yourself. Hiking can be a constant lesson in sensing, on many levels. You can become highly attuned to what is going on around you as well as inside of you, sensing subtle changes in the weather and landscape while at the same time listening to the quiet wisdom of your body.

Hiking is where everything you've been practicing comes together: your technique, your wisdom, your planning, and your inner work, along with your ability to focus and relax to conserve energy.

Not all walkers are hikers, but all hikers *are* walkers, so most of the same basic focuses for walking apply to hiking. However, with hiking, the variable terrain, the steep inclines, the extra weight you may be carrying, and being out in Nature require an extra set of tools and knowledge. What we'll cover in this chapter is how to make your movement through Nature a safe and healthy experience. Here's an overview of the chapter:

- The Five Mindful Steps
- Preparing for your hike
- Clothing choices
- ChiWalking technique specific to hiking
- Fueling
- Hydration
- Hiking in heat and cold
- Carrying weight

THE FIVE MINDFUL STEPS

Whether you're new to hiking or a seasoned veteran who wants to learn better technique, the Five Mindful Steps are a great way to get yourself going in the best direction. Here's how they apply to hiking:

GET ALIGNED

Your first job is to get aligned with hiking and the added effort it requires, both mentally and physically. For most of us, going for a hike is not as simple as walking out our door. It requires some forethought and planning. Hiking asks us to take on a certain mind-set—to have a strong intent, with which we must first get aligned. Once we're out in Nature, it serves us to get aligned with the rhythms of Nature and the quiet that surrounds us. By combining an awareness of your long, strong, straight spine with deep belly breathing, you'll find that you can easily become aligned with and relate to the beauty surrounding you.

ENGAGE YOUR CORE

When hiking, you need to engage your core even more in order to handle rougher terrain and to bear the extra weight you might be carrying. Leveling your pelvis while hiking helps to relieve pressure on your lower back while also keeping your stride stable and centered.

It is also by engaging our core that we can feel ourselves more profoundly. Every time you engage your core physically, you are pulling on a deeper aspect of who you are. Hiking in Nature is a wonderful time to feel your Self in relation to the huge vastness of Nature.

CREATE BALANCE

Hiking demands a much greater ability to maintain centeredness in your movement. Rocks, roots, stream crossings, and narrow trails demand that you be responsive and balanced on your feet. It is a great way to build a clearer sense of balance and self-confidence, which you can then transfer into any challenging situation.

It is also important to create balance in your hiking program. If you like to take long hikes periodically, be sure to keep your walking program in balance by doing weekly hikes to keep your body in shape for those longer ones. If you don't, you could be overworking muscles that are not used to that level of duration and intensity, possibly throwing your entire fitness program out of balance.

Another aspect of balance you will recognize while hiking is the perfect balance of Nature from which we all can learn. While walking in Nature, you have the opportunity to study how beautifully everything in Nature blends together and works in a balanced way. Watching the abundance of harmony in Nature can drive you deeply into recognizing what is most out of balance in your own life. It's amazing what comes to the surface when you have the time and space to feel your Self and listen to your thoughts. Hiking is definitely my favorite time to ponder my life and think about how I can create more balance and sanity in it.

MAKE A CHOICE

While hiking, your choices become more profound and more serious. I have chosen paths and trails that have taken me far off-course and made me aware, all too clearly, of the importance of making wise choices—for instance, deciding once to take a shortcut by climbing up a cliff, only to get to a place where going up or back down was equally terrifying. I survived but realized my choice of climbing up was foolhardy and selfish as I had others with me whom I had also put at risk.

There are always lots of wonderful choices to make: which type of view you might want to see, how long to meander around the lake, what peak to climb. In Nature, as in hiking, I delight in the incredible freedom I feel, to make my own choices—and learn from them. The key here is knowing what you want but taking the conditions into account when making your choices. Better wise than weary.

MOVE FORWARD

Hiking is about getting yourself out the door and into Nature, as well as keeping your forward movement steady and consistent, whether it is a 30-minute hike or an all-day trek. Once you've *chosen* your destination, the final "step" is to take the first step! Get moving, go out, and enjoy the challenge and the beauty of hiking. You'll be amazed at how much is out there for you to discover—internally *and* externally.

PREPARING FOR YOUR HIKE

First and foremost with hiking, it is important to be physically prepared for the hike you've chosen. You can most definitely go out on a short Nature hike that is flat and slightly rolling at any stage in your fitness program, but as soon as you get into longer hikes and trails of more difficulty, you need to apply the principle of Gradual Progress and slowly build up to higher levels of difficulty and duration. Too many people lose the joy of hiking in Nature by pushing themselves too hard and too far.

In preparing for a hike, you also need to make sure you have what you need for the duration of the hike. One difference between walking and hiking is the amount of stuff you take along. The number of items you take with you is directly proportional to the length of time you intend to be out. A short hike might require no more than you would normally take with you on a typical walk: a water bottle, a hat, and a jacket. On the other hand, a 4-hour hike will take a bit more planning and most likely require a day pack to hold everything. When you're hiking, you have to leave behind a lot of conveniences like roofs, restrooms, and Starbucks, so I've made up a little checklist to go over when you're heading out past the pavement.

THE SHORT LIST

To Do
- ❑ plan your route
- ❑ check the local weather
- ❑ dress appropriately
- ❑ leave a "flight plan" and estimated time of return if you're hiking alone
- ❑ eat a light meal at least an hour before you begin your hike
- ❑ hydrate the day before and drink 12 ounces of water before heading out

To Bring (depending on how long you'll be out)
- ❑ day pack or fanny pack
- ❑ sunscreen, ChapStick
- ❑ layered clothing
- ❑ windbreaker jacket (preferably waterproof), a vest, or a small packable poncho
- ❑ water bottle
- ❑ electrolyte replacement (capsules or powdered mix)
- ❑ fuel (food, snacks, sports bars, Gu, Clif Shot, et cetera)
- ❑ pocket knife (I prefer a Swiss Army knife with tweezers)
- ❑ hat (for cold or sun) or bandanna
- ❑ map (if necessary)
- ❑ fully charged cell phone (leave it turned off, use for emergencies only)
- ❑ good hiking shoes or boots
- ❑ Band-Aids
- ❑ cushioned wicking socks and an extra pair of dry socks (packed in a Ziploc bag)
- ❑ duct tape (I've used it more times than I can count)

KNOW WHERE YOU'RE GOING

Before heading out the door, be sure to familiarize yourself with where you're going to be hiking. If you're going into new territory, get a map of the area and go over the lay of the land so that you can be better prepared for anything that might come up.

The best advice I can give anyone who is into doing extended hikes is to learn how to read and follow United States Geological Survey topographic maps. They are generally very accurate and will tell you just about everything you need to know about a given area. There is an incredible Web site for this. It will show you aerial photos taken from satellites of almost any area of the United States. You can then magnify the view to see extraordinary details of topography—right down to individual trees! The site gives you the choice of viewing an aerial photo or a topographic map of the same shot. You can see an overview of the area through which you might want to hike and then download a map of where you're going. It's pretty convenient, and very cool (http://terraserver-usa.com/).

CHECK THE WEATHER

A sunny day can change quickly in many climes, and cold, rainy weather can turn hot and sunny. Both are hazards if you're not prepared. The quickest way to check the weather is on the Internet.

TAKE WHAT YOU'LL NEED

When planning a hike the best policy is to visualize in your mind doing the hike and think about everything you might need while you're out there. If it's familiar terrain and you've hiked it before, plan and pack accordingly. Either check over the list above or come up with your own list of items you can't live without, and take everything you think you'll need and are willing to carry.

Plan your supplies and energy expenditures for the day. What are the characteristics of the hike you're planning? Will your start be mostly uphill, with a downhill return, or will you be going downhill first and then climbing back up for the second half of your hike? A seemingly small detail like this could make a huge difference in what you take with you.

CLOTHING CHOICES

Anything you wear hiking should be loose-fitting and comfortable. Light nylon or polyester clothing dries rapidly and stays lightweight when wet. It doesn't snag as easily and compresses well in a pack. I may be old-fashioned, but I prefer to wear light cotton even though it's impractical for many reasons: it doesn't wick moisture away from your body; it doesn't dry quickly; and it gets heavy when wet. It collects seed spikes easily and it doesn't compress or pack small. But it doesn't feel like plastic either.

For many, layering is the most effective way to dress for the outdoors. By wearing various layers of clothing, you can regulate your body temperature and avoid having too much or too little body heat. Here's a crash course in layering. When you're packing your clothes, just think of the four *W*'s: wicking, warming, windproofing, and waterproofing. Depending on your hike, you'll need one or more of these types of clothing along with you. Here's a rundown of these four clothing groups:

- *Wicking* clothing draws moisture away from your skin, which keeps you drier and less susceptible to chafing. In colder weather, it's very important to stay dry if you want to stay warm. These clothes are usually thin and close-fitting. You can use either polyester fiber, which wicks well and dries quickly, or, if you don't like the feel of plastic, you can opt for silk (my choice), which works just as well and is a natural fiber.
- *Warming* clothing is usually lightweight but woven in a way that traps a lot of air, providing a layer of insulation on top of the wicking layer. Most polyester fleece clothing does a great job of this and also offers additional wicking. Wool does the trick as well but weighs a bit more.
- *Windproofing* clothing is usually thin and lightweight. Just a shell is all you need. There are microfiber shirts and jackets out now that look and feel like nice soft pliable cloth. They cut the wind extremely well, yet are breathable enough to allow some evaporation to escape.

- **_Waterproof_** clothing is great if you're expecting to get rained on. The drawback to any piece of rainwear labeled _waterproof_ is that it doesn't breathe. That means that when you're wearing it, moisture cannot escape from your body. If you're hiking in a rain jacket, you'll get sweaty pretty quickly. My experience with hiking in rain gear is that I end up getting as wet on the inside as I would if I didn't have it on. It does, however, hold in heat and keep out wind. I usually go for wearing a jacket labeled _water-repellent_ or _water-resistant_, which has some water repellency mixed with some breathability, and then hope I don't run into a downpour. For better ventilation, many of the higher-end jackets now have a number of ways to vent the coat without opening the front zipper. The backs are vented and there are additional zippers in the armpits to release excess heat and moisture.

The best way to learn how to layer properly is to experiment. No one knows your body like you do, so keep these four types of clothing in your "hiking closet" and see which combination works best for the way you hike. When packing for a hike, think ahead and take only what you're sure you'll need. Every body demands an individual comfort level while hiking, so clothing choices can fall somewhere between spartan and excessive. Check the local weather and pack accordingly.

LEAVE A "FLIGHT PLAN"

If you plan to hike alone, always write down a description of your planned hike along with an estimated return time and leave it with a friend or on your car windshield as you leave the trailhead. It could save your life.

STAY IN TOUCH

Most of the items on the packing list are self-explanatory, but I do suggest taking a cell phone. Some of you may groan, but for safety purposes there is nothing better. Sometimes you won't get reception in mountainous areas, but many new-generation cell phones come equipped with a GPS signal that you can switch to when you're out of range. Check out your owner's manual to see if your phone has this feature. Make sure your phone is fully charged and leave it off unless an emergency comes up—and I don't mean calling ahead for Chinese takeout on your way home from the trailhead.

WHAT ELSE?

Duct tape! Yes, that's right, good ol' duct tape. This amazing miracle of modern man is good to have with you on longer hikes. A small thing to carry and really helpful when you need it, it's good for anything from preventing blisters to healing bad zippers—and you never know when your water bottle will start leaking. It's also great for preventing chafing.

Take it off the huge spool it comes on and "roll your own" around a small length of pencil to conserve space. Stick some on your feet if you start to get "hot spots." Many ultra marathoners and adventure racers swear by it. If this doesn't work, you can always fall back on the old standbys like Band-Aids and moleskin, which I also suggest carrying. But duct tape lasts longer and is multipurpose.

ChiWalking Technique Specific to Hiking

- **Align yourself and engage your core.** Chances are that you'll be carrying more with you when you're hiking than when you're walking, so the first adjustment you'll need to make is with your posture. When walking with weight on your back it is crucial that you allow as much of the weight of the pack as possible to be supported by your legs and not by your back. This means that you'll have to engage your core muscles to stabilize your pelvis and your spine. Leveling your pelvis and flattening your back is what does the trick. This will also help you to keep your upper body forward, over your feet.
- **Lean *into* the hills.** Don't let the incline of the hill throw you back onto your heels. If you do, you'll be reaching up the hill ahead of your center of gravity, thus causing your hamstrings to pull you up the hill. Leveling your pelvis and leaning up the hill will ensure that you stay over your feet with each step and that you're pushing yourself up the hill, not pulling yourself. The best way to lean for-

ward is from your ankles, not from your waist (which can put a strain on your lower back). If you are holding your pelvis level as you hike, this won't be a problem because when your pelvis is level, you *can't* bend at the waist. Try this experiment:

Figure 59a—Incorrect: walking with upper body too vertical

Figure 59b—Correct: leaning forward from the ankles

- Stand up tall, with your best posture.
- Tilt your pelvis *down* in front. This will disengage your core muscles and give you an anterior pelvic tilt, a swayback.
- Now bend over at the waist and your upper body will flop over forward effortlessly.
- Come back upright and stand again with your best posture, except this time level your pelvis and hold it level, using your lower abdominals.
- Now, if you try to bend over at the waist, you'll see that as long as your pelvis is level, you can't bend. Keeping your pelvis level in this way will keep your core muscles engaged, creating much more power in your legs.

- **Keep your heels down** at all times unless you're climbing something so steep that you have to use your hands. When the terrain gets steep enough to put you onto your toes, turn your body sideways to the hill and walk up with a lateral stride. As you turn your feet sideways to the hill, the angle of your ankle opens up and your Achilles tendons can relax. Allowing your heels to remain in con-

Figure 60a—Lateral stride: Step 1. Bring left heel even with right toe

Figure 60b—Step 2. Take a short step uphill with the right foot

Figure 60c—Step 3. Bring left heel even with right toe

Figure 60d—Step 4. Take a short step uphill with the right foot

tact with the ground will take an enormous amount of work off of your lower legs and possibly spare you any calf pulls or shin splints.

- **Keep your hands free** when you're hiking. You'll need them for stability and to catch yourself, should you trip or slide. When I'm walking in very rough terrain I like to wear cycling gloves, the ones with padded palms and half-length mesh fingers. You can still have your bare fingers free to fiddle with stuff, but your palms are covered with padded leather in case you go down.

- **Maintain a comfortable, steady pace** and stop as infrequently as possible. As Colin Fletcher says in his book *The Complete Walker IV*: "... the most important single element in the physical act of walking is *rhythm.*" This doesn't necessarily mean that you'll always be walking with the same rhythm. It means that one should walk rhythmically, without interruption. At times the terrain might dictate that you have to step more frequently or with shorter strides, but by maintaining a sense of continual movement, without lots of little disruptions, your legs will be able to carry you for much longer stretches. Start your hike slowly and search for your optimal gait and rhythm. I can usually settle into a very efficient and comfortable pace if I imagine that I'm setting out to walk for 24 hours without stopping.

- **Synch your breathing with your stride.** For most of my hiking, I exhale for 2 steps and inhale for 1. You should experiment with your breath and find a breathing rhythm that feels effortless without leaving you breathless. The reason why 2:1 works for me is that each time I breathe out, I'm stepping on a different foot, whereas, if I were to walk with a 2:2 breath rate, I'd be always exhaling on the same leg, creating the possibility of walking with an asymmetrical stride. It may sound picky, but in terms of efficiency, every little tweak helps. Actually, keeping a 2:1 rhythm allows your walking to take on the flavor of a waltz. Now isn't that a nice way to go through a forest?

  Experiment with your breath rate and always allow it to adjust to your exertion level. It's different for different people depending on their level of conditioning and efficiency. When you walk faster or uphill, you'll have to breathe a little faster to supply your legs with more oxygen. If you're hiking at high altitude, it helps immensely to belly breathe while hiking. It gets a much larger volume of air into your lungs and will consequently help to increase your blood-oxygen level as you head into higher realms (see Belly Breathing, page 52).

Some people have a tendency to get uptight when their breath rate increases. It's absolutely *normal* that your breath rate increases during exercise—that's why you're out there! When you're first getting into walking, your breath rate could be faster because you're not aerobically conditioned. Not to worry. After a month of consistent walking, you'll be breathing much more comfortably. When you're trying to improve your aerobic level, it's not so much about walking fast as it is about walking for longer periods of time.

Synchronizing my breathing with my footsteps actually brings a meditative quality into my hiking, and watching my breath is always a great way to keep my mind from overworking when I'm out in Nature (see *Meditative Walk* in chapter 5).

- **Shorten your stride on the uphills.** As you encounter any increase in the amount of slope you're walking on, allow your stride to shorten accordingly. The easiest way to naturally shorten your stride is to relax your legs so they won't swing as far with each step.
- **Increase your arm swing.** In addition to shortening your stride as the hills get steeper, I recommend increasing the force of your arm swing at the same time. The idea is to take some of the workload off of your legs and transfer it to your upper body with a bigger arm swing. Bend your arms to 90° and swing them forward and upward with each stride. Begin each arm swing with your hands at your hips and finish each swing with your hands up near your chin. And don't forget to swing with a good deal of chutzpah. Hiking hills can be a great upper body workout too!

HIKING UP STEEP HILLS

Many people tend to shy away from hiking steep terrain, complaining that it's so much work. Well, I'm here to put all those fears to rest by saying that hiking steep hills isn't that much harder than hiking flat terrain—if you can learn how to use your "gears."

- **Use your gears.** What do you do when you go up a steep hill in your car? You downshift. Right? You go to a smaller gear so that the engine doesn't have to work as hard to push or pull your car up the hill. So the easiest way to get your body up steep hills is to follow the same laws of physics that apply to your car. Changing to a shorter, quicker stride acts in much the same way as downshifting to a lower gear. Taking smaller steps means that you are not having to lift your body as far vertically with each step, so each step of the climb won't be as tiring.

- **Increase your arm swing.** This should be an integral part of any decrease in your stride length due to the steepness of a hill. Follow the advice given previously.

- **Slow down.** Your speed will naturally decrease a bit, but who's in a hurry to get up those steepest hills? Not me. The easiest way to naturally shorten your stride is to relax your legs and they won't swing as far with each step. Above all, try to always conserve your leg strength on uphills, because that's where you burn the most fuel. If you're hiking for long distances uphill, you should plan accordingly and keep your stride generally shorter and as relaxed as possible so that you'll still have some energy left in your legs when you reach the top. You're going to need it on the way back down.

- **Snap your knees.** Here's another tip for the steep sections. When I was training for the Leadville 100-mile Endurance Run, I discovered this great way to walk up steep hills efficiently. I eventually ended up hiking about 25 miles of the race, so this discovery was a godsend for tired legs. I realized that if I stepped up the hill ahead of myself, it would cause me to use too much hamstring to pull myself up the hill. I found instead that when I could keep my stride very short with my feet stepping up underneath my center of gravity, I could move up the mountain by simply straightening my knees, one after the other. It takes relatively little muscle to straighten your legs and it makes climbing steep hills a snap.

HIKING DOWN STEEP HILLS

There's a real art to hiking down steep slopes without hammering your quads or trashing your knees along the way. The secret is in learning how to *reduce your impact with the ground.* This theme should always be in the front of your mind whenever you find yourself heading down a steep trail. The jarring motion of pounding down a steep descent wreaks havoc with even the best hikers' legs. Here are a few things you can do to soften your impact and ease your way down even the most difficult pitches:

- **Shorten your stride.** The same rule that works for steep uphills holds true for the steep downhills. By taking shorter steps, your body will not gain as much speed with each stride, so there is naturally less force created as your foot meets the ground. This adds up to *less impact* on your knees and quads. Also, pick up your feet and take shorter, quicker steps rolling heel-to-toe to cushion the impact even more.

- **Level your pelvis.** Another area of your body to watch out for on steep downhills is your lower back. A lot of compression can occur along your spine every time the weight of your body meets the ground. For those of us with any lower back or spinal issues, the thought of pounding down a steep hill doesn't sound very

Figure 61a—Incorrect: pelvis not level, so stress goes to the lower back

Figure 61b—Correct: pelvis level; lower your tailbone going down the hill appealing. Here's a great way to avoid compressing any vertebrae while descending a steep slope. Level your pelvis, just as you do in the posture exercise. As you pick up your pubic bone with your lower abdominals, your lower back will flatten out, thus increasing the space between the discs along your lower spine.

Try This Exercise
1. Stand at the top of a steep slope with your feet pointed forward and knees slightly bent in a Grounding Stance.
2. Drop your tailbone toward your heels. This will level your pelvis and engage your lower abdominals. Imagine an invisible line connecting your tailbone to your heels and pretend that you're sitting on an invisible one-legged stool. If you soften your knees and bounce slightly up and down, you should be able to feel pressure on your heels. Keep your posture vertical and directly over your ankles.
3. Walk in place by lightly picking up your knees.
4. Now walk down the hill picking up your knees and lowering yourself down onto your heels with each step. If you're doing it right, you should feel like you're going down the hill on an escalator.
5. If you want to walk downhill faster, simply pick up your knees faster but keep your stride short.

- **Watch the ground.** There's nothing more disconcerting than slipping on a steep slope. Patches of loose dirt and gravel can turn any downhill hike into a nightmare. The best way to stay on your feet is to carefully pick the spots where your feet are going to come down.

  I know what you're thinking—"There's not a whole lot of time to think between footsteps"—and you're right. There isn't. But with a little practice you can easily develop the necessary skills. Here are a couple of tips that will make the decision-making process much quicker and easier on those slippery slopes.

1. Look for grass or vegetation along the edges of the trail. In most cases there's a lot more traction on grass than on dirt, so stay on the grass when you need to.

2. Look for exposed rock. Any rock that is at least half buried is not going to move when you step on it. As long as you've got decent traction on the soles of your shoes, your foot won't go anywhere if it meets solid rock. I'm constantly looking for any little rocks that stick out of the trail and as long as *any* part of my shoe sole comes to rest on a solid rock, my odds of slipping go way down.

3. If you're hiking down the middle of a very narrow V-shaped drainage, you can straddle the path and create enough cross-pressure to hold your foot on the path without slipping.

4. Always keep an eye on what's coming up ahead of you. Be aware of upcoming flat spots in the trail where you can "bail out" if your downhill speed gets carried away. If a trail is particularly steep and tricky, I take it in short sections, stopping at the end of each section to plan my next series of steps. It's no time to be in a hurry.

5. If a steep downhill trail has vegetation growing along the sides, I'll often hold on to overhanging tree branches or low-growing bushes, slowing down my speed as I go by.

6. When all else fails, you can always sidestep your way down a steep slope.

Hiking down a steep slope can be scary if you don't know what to do. The more you practice these tools, the less likely those steep descents will throw you off your stride.

FUELING

This is a very misunderstood subject. There is so much information out there that it's hard to tell what to follow. So I've come up with a few good working rules and their respective explanations. Here are a few guidelines for proper fueling:

1. Take along lightweight, simple-carbohydrate foods that digest easily. If your blood sugar gets low, you'll need a fast-acting food that will get into your bloodstream right away. Fruits are a great

source of simple carbohydrates. Energy bars contain complex carbohydrates which will digest more slowly.

2. If you plan to go for a long, strenuous day hike, you can do what any good athlete would do before a big event—carbo loading. When I'm preparing for an ultradistance event, I begin my race diet 6 days out from the event by eating high-protein meals for the first 3 days and then switching to high-carbohydrate meals for the last 3 days.

3. It's best not to eat while walking. Stop and take the time to ingest your food, chewing it well. It will get into your bloodstream more quickly.

4. For early-morning hikes of 2 hours or less, it can be great to do your hike on an empty stomach and work up a healthy appetite. When you're done, you can reward yourself with a healthy, delicious meal. Do whatever you can to avoid coming back and tanking up on candy, soda, and fast foods. Healthy food really has its place after a good hike and can be an nice integral part of your hiking ritual.

5. For hikes of more than 2 hours, have a healthy carbohydrate breakfast at least an hour before taking off. Avoid eating heavy proteins like eggs and meat before hiking, as they are slow to digest and can cause you to feel sluggish while hiking. When you return from your hike you can eat a good protein-carbohydrate meal for lunch or dinner to rebuild your muscle tissues and replenish your glycogen stores.

HYDRATION

I can't emphasize enough how important it is to drink water before, during, and after hiking—or any exercise, for that matter. Our bodies are about 50 percent to 65 percent water, which should suggest how any variance from that range could affect how your body works. Drinking water while hiking is mainly to replace sweat. The evaporative quality of sweat keeps your body cool during exercise.

When it comes to hiking, the biggest issue to watch for is dehydration, which can definitely reduce the quality of your hikes. As you sweat, you not only lose water, but you also lose valuable salts (electrolytes) and minerals from your system. Electrolytes are what help your muscle cells to function properly. If you sweat enough salts out of your system, it will create an electrolyte imbalance in your muscle tissues, causing the onset of cramps. No fun. So it is not only important to drink plenty of water while hiking, it's important to drink water containing electrolytes. There are many electrolyte-replacement drinks (sports drinks) on the market, and it is worth your while to study their ingredients to make sure they're doing the right thing. Many drinks contain high amounts of sugar, which can upset the acid balance in your stomach if consumed in excessively large quantities. As a rule, I don't like to put any chemical in my body that isn't close to a naturally occurring substance. Potassium, sodium, and calcium are three electrolytes that I'm used to having in my body, so I use electrolyte-replacement capsules and take one every hour while exercising. I try to avoid sports drinks that have a label that looks like a chemistry final.

A fast hiker can sweat as much as 16 ounces of water per hour. This means that she should be drinking water at regular intervals to avoid dehydration. The average person who burns 2,000 calories a day should drink 2 to 3 quarts of water daily. You can adjust this number to fit your needs. If you think you burn more calories per day, you can add roughly 36 ounces of water for each additional 1,000 calories you burn. Water does it all. It helps transport metabolic waste out of your muscles. It is a part of the conversion of muscle glycogen into energy. It is a large component of sweat, which helps to cool the body during exercise.

CARRYING WEIGHT

Since this chapter is about hiking technique, I'm going to take some poetic license here and limit my coverage of hiking to any outing that can be done in a day. For overnight instructions you'll have to go talk to Colin Fletcher. He's the expert in long-range planning, equipment, and all the other aspects of backpacking.

Everything that you could possibly need in a day hike should fill no more than a day pack. So when it comes to carrying weight, the most I can imagine carrying on a one-day trip would be 15 to 20 pounds tops, unless you're a terminal rock hound with a greedy streak.

As far as hiking with weight is concerned, let physics be your guide.

- When your daypack is on your back, it should hang close to your spine. The muscles in your legs and back will work a lot less if the center of gravity of your pack lies close to your own center of gravity.

- Constantly remind yourself to hold your pelvis level. This will keep your posture aligned and allow your *structure* to bear your weight instead of your *muscles*.

- Walk with shorter strides when carrying weight. Longer strides will slow down your cadence and force you to bear weight on each leg for a longer period of time, thus tiring you more quickly.

- Balance the contents in your pack so that the heavier items are closer to your centerline and your spine. Lighter items can be distributed throughout the rest of the pack.

- Cinch your waistband so that the pack doesn't shift back and forth with each step you take. It not only wears out your legs faster, it can be very unsafe if you lose your balance.

If you find that you end up carrying a lot of weight, you might think of investing in a good internal-frame day pack with a padded waist belt. This wonderful piece of equipment will transfer most of the weight from your shoulders to your hips, where it should be.

For the rest of us who like to carry the basic necessities, any good, well-fitting lightweight day pack will do just fine. If you're thinking of buying a day pack for hiking, do your own research first by asking for recommendations from friends or by picking the brains of the salespeople at your nearest outdoor store. First and foremost, when you go shopping for a good pack, make sure that it's a comfortable fit. When you find a pack you like, look around for some heavy objects and stuff the pack with some weight so that you can tell what it feels like with a load. Is it still comfortable? Tighten up the waist belt and check to see if the pack moves around when you twist your body side to side. It should feel snug and comfortable around your body and not be restrictive in any way. If you can Body Sense your way through the process of buying a day pack, you can't go wrong.

Other amenities to look for in a pack include compartments to hold things. It helps to be able to quickly find whatever it is that you might need, so that you don't have to stop and dig through the entire pack. A good pack should have separate compartments for clothing, toiletries, food, and maps, and a convenient sleeve for a water bottle. Compression straps are great for shrinking the volume of the pack so that the contents hang closer to your center of gravity. External straps and loops for additional tie-ons are a plus. Heavy-duty waterproof nylon is a must, as is a good, sturdy bottom that won't wear through after the first season. I used to sew my own parkas for hiking, so I always look to see how well the pack is stitched together. Look on the inside of the pack. Are the seams rough or are they taped and sealed? The pack should look just as beautiful turned inside out. If it doesn't, it's questionable how long the seams will last. The shoulder straps should be wide and well padded. An adjustable chest strap running between the shoulder straps helps to keep the weight of the pack from digging into your shoulders.

Day packs can be pricey, but the good ones are worth it. If you use a day pack often, you know that it is not the place to scrimp on cost. Quality rules!

HIKING IN HEAT AND COLD

Common sense will get you a long way when it comes to hiking in temperature extremes. I'll cover the obvious tips and also leave you with some you hadn't discovered yet.

IN THE COLD

One of the most challenging things about hiking in the cold is making the right clothing choices. Ideally, you want to have just enough clothing on that your body temperature stays at a nice medium level—not too hot and not too cold. If you get too hot, you'll start to sweat and your clothing will get soaked from the inside out. Then as soon as you stop moving, your body temperature will drop because you're no longer producing extra body heat *and* you're standing around in wet clothes. That's not a good combination and can result in hypothermia. That's why it's very important to regulate your body heat while hiking in the cold.

The two areas of your body that work best to regulate your body temperature are your head and your throat. If you cover either of them, you'll retain more heat. That's why turtlenecks and wool hats were invented.

Wool hats can sometimes get a little itchy, so I've switched to woven polyester winter caps or a polyester-wool blend. I've even seen wool hats with a polyester band that goes across your forehead. These are my favorite. They wick moisture away from your head, they don't lose their stretch when they get wet, and they're lightweight. They also pack small in case you end up taking the hat off and having to stow it.

The most versatile top to wear, in my opinion, is a long-sleeved turtleneck with wicking ability that zips open in front. When you feel yourself getting too warm, you can simply zip down the collar and let a little cold air onto your neck. You can also push up the sleeves when you need cooling off.

Another favorite piece of heat-regulating clothing is my nylon shell vest. It has a very high collar that covers my neck when I need it and packs to a minuscule size if I don't need it. I can wear it under a sweater or fleece jacket, and it keeps my core temperature just right through a wide range of conditions.

In order to hike with a comfortable body temperature it's best to layer your clothing, which I have previously mentioned.

When you're hiking in the cold, you can also control your body heat by adjusting your level of exertion. If you're feeling chilled, you can always pick up the pace a little until your body heat increases.

Another thing to practice while hiking in cooler temperatures is *relaxing* while you're walking. When you're relaxed, blood circulates through your muscles more easily, providing you with plenty of heat and keeping your core warm.

HIKING IN THE HEAT

Keeping your body temperature cool while hiking in the heat is always a challenge. When the humidity is high it is even more difficult because your body depends on evaporating sweat for cooling. And when it's humid, less sweat will evaporate from your skin. But I would say that the most important body part to keep cool while hiking in the heat is your brain. If the temperature of your brain rises even a couple of degrees, its ability to work optimally decreases. Whenever I'm hiking in very hot weather I make it a point to keep water on my head. I also suggest wearing a lightweight, breathable running hat, preferably a white one, which will reflect heat. A good, wide-brimmed straw hat also works well to keep the sun off your back and shoulders while circulating plenty of air through the crown.

Slow down your speed to keep perspiration low and above all *don't focus on the heat* or you'll become worn down by it. Be aware of it, but relate to it in a friendly way. Set your countdown timer to remind you to drink a mouthful of water every 10 minutes. This will ensure that you keep drinking the right amount of fluid and replacing your electrolytes on a regular basis. I take an electrolyte capsule every 45 minutes if I'm exercising in hot weather and I set my second countdown timer to make sure it happens. Electrolytes taken with sweets can aid in increasing the absorption rate of water into your system. That's why many electrolyte replacement drinks contain some glucose or fructose.

I've already explained some of the reasons why I prefer to use electrolyte capsules instead of carrying a sports drink, but here are a few more reasons:

- The capsules are small and easy to pack.
- I can always carry something sweet with me to help keep my blood sugar good.
- I can almost *always* find a source of water.
- I can't always find a source of electrolyte drinks. If I'm hiking in the mountains and all I've brought is my favorite ready-mix sports drink, what happens when I drink the last drop and I've still got 10 miles to go? It's worth thinking about; muscle cramps are *really* no fun.

I tend to look at trail walking as a paradigm for life. The people who get the best views are the ones willing to take the risks to get there. You can enjoy walking whether or not you like to hike. But I highly recommend hiking for any of you with an adventurous spirit and an appreciation of Nature. I guarantee it'll take your walking into another dimension.

CHAPTER NINE

Indoor Walking and the Mindful Treadmill

Everywhere is walking distance, if you have the time.
—STEVEN WRIGHT

'm an outdoors nut when it comes to exercise. I like to breathe fresh air and feel spaciousness around me when I'm working out. There's no doubt about it—there's more available energy in Nature than there ever will be inside any building. That being said, there are definitely times when an indoor venue is exactly what is called for. For those of you living in the colder northern climates, walking indoors in the wintertime can be a relief from trudging through six inches or more of frozen slush. If you live in the inner city where air pollution and personal safety are big concerns, having an indoor space to walk any time you choose can be comforting. If you live in a very hot or humid climate, the luxury of having an air-conditioned place to walk can be an absolute godsend. Or, you might be on a business trip and so squeezed for time that you can't afford the time it takes to go somewhere else and walk.

This chapter is intended as an alternative guide for those times when heading outdoors is either not an option or not very appealing. You should never want for a good workout as long as you're willing and creative.

Here are some of the options we'll cover in this chapter:

- Treadmill walking
- Mall walking (sorry: no shopping)
- Climbing stairs
- Parking garages
- Gyms
- Indoor tracks
- Airports

TREADMILL WALKING

We'll start with the treadmill because it is the best of all the indoor alternatives. That's because treadmills offer an excellent way to get a nice walk without any interruption in your rhythm and flow. I will, however, preface this section by saying again that there is no equivalent alternative to walking outdoors, where the challenges of everyday life can definitely add a deeper dimension to your walking. Walking in the snow and rain or along a busy sidewalk can be both beautiful and challenging. And you can luxuriate in a nice hot bath afterward, absolutely guilt-free.

Challenges are good for you. Dodging puddles, poodles, and people can give your lateral muscles a workout that a treadmill never can. Outdoor walking builds a level of character and inner strength that treadmills can't match. What I'm getting at is that if a treadmill is always your first choice, you could be limiting yourself in many ways.

Also be aware that treadmill walking is fundamentally different than outdoor walking because on the treadmill you are walking on top of a moving platform, not a stationary surface, so your heels are meeting a moving object coming at you. As your speed increases, so does the impact on your heels. Therefore, walking on the treadmill should be done mostly at an aerobic pace. Faster walks can be done, but keep them short and listen closely to your body for any counterindications that might come up. Following these simple steps will ensure that every treadmill workout is a good one.

- Transition into your treadmill walk. Practice your posture stance for a couple of minutes before getting on the treadmill. It's much easier to instate good posture habits if you do it before you begin moving. Then the first thing you do as you begin your walk is to check in with your postural alignment while it is still fresh in your body memory.
- If you're in a gym and unfamiliar with the operation of the treadmill, ask someone to help you with the basics. Be sure you know how to stop the machine. If it's a programmable machine, familiarize yourself with enough of the operations so that you can either choose from a selection of workouts or make up your own. This will ensure that you can always create some variety in your workouts.
- Stand on the stationary side rails of the treadmill and start the machine at a low speed. Step onto the machine and begin walking at a very slow pace. Start out at 18 to 20 minutes per mile.
- Many treadmills in gyms are positioned in front of large wall mirrors. I have found this to be somewhat disorienting because there isn't anything to focus on except a reflection in the mirror. To solve this problem, I place a sticky note right on the mirror, in front of my face, centered at eye level so that I have a nonmoving object as my focal point. It might sound a little nutty, but it makes a huge difference when I'm on the treadmill for more than 20 minutes.

Being internally focused and having a good visual focal point will keep you from being distracted. Gyms are busy with people moving and exercising and checking each other out. It's a prime place to be pulled off your center, so having a focal point is always a good reminder to return to your center, no matter what's going on around you.

- Every manufacturer uses different numbers, speeds, and settings, so follow the readout display to see how fast you're walking. If it tells you minutes per mile, that's all you really need.
- Start at what feels like a slow pace and very gradually work your way up to whatever speed you'll be eventually walking. Listen to your body for when to increase the speed. If your breath rate or heart rate increases too rapidly, drop your speed a notch and stay at the slower speed for a few minutes until your rhythm and pace feel steady and relaxed. If your breath rate and heart rate *don't* go up, you'll need to make friends with the "+" button. Remember, it's a *work*out. So if work isn't happening on some level, there will also be no change going on.

THREE TREADMILL WORKOUTS

Some machines have preprogrammed workouts requiring various degrees of exertion. These are good to try once you've gotten used to walking on the treadmill and you feel comfortable with changing the speed and incline of the ramp. I've always been a big fan of varying the workouts. If you walk on a treadmill a lot, or have one at home, it's a great way to keep your approach fresh. Here are three basic treadmill workouts that can function as themes to which you can add your own personal touches and variations. Try out each one and see what you could do to custom fit them to your personal walking needs.

The Aerobic Workout

Since the object of an aerobic workout is to keep your body within your aerobic zone, it's best to know what your aerobic speed is. As a rule of thumb, it should be fast enough that you can carry on a conversation, but are *just* able to. If you were to go any faster, your breathing would be too heavy for you to speak comfortably. This is a bent-arm workout and for most people the cadence will fall within the 65 to 70 spm range. If you use a heart rate monitor, your target heart rate should be $220 - (\text{your age}) \times .6 = \text{Target Heart Rate}$. Hold this speed for as long as it feels comfortable and doesn't cause any stress on your legs. If you're just starting a walking program on the treadmill, walk until you're comfortably tired, then stop and note the amount of time you spent on the treadmill. When you return for your next aerobic workout, walk for that same amount of time and, at the end, check in with your body to see if you can handle another 5 minutes. If you don't hear any disagreement from your body, go for it. But if there is any discomfort, skip it until next time. Don't increase the length of your aerobic workout more than once in a week. I recommend two aerobic walks per week. These walks should be your longest walks, and you can gradually build up to any length of time that feels physically comfortable, doable.

The Cardio Workout

Doing a cardiovascular workout on a treadmill is risky at best. I say that because in order to get a good cardiovascular workout you'll need to be walking faster to get your heart rate up. There is no way around it. The problem with a treadmill is that as the speed increases, so does the impact to your legs. So how do you strengthen your heart without sacrificing your legs? The easiest solution is to increase your speed so that your heart rate increases and then hold that speed for periods of time long enough to get your heart rate up but brief enough to keep your legs under the "injury threshold." I usually hold a faster speed for 1 minute and then drop my speed back to the former level. Then after a minute of easier walking I'll do another minute of fast walking. For the entire workout I'll alternate between a minute of fast walking and a minute of slow walking. They're called treadmill intervals.

- Start slowly and warm up to a comfortable aerobic pace with your cadence at around 63 to 65 spm.
- Preset your countdown timer to beep every minute (or check the clock on the wall). After you've warmed up and held your cadence steady for 10 minutes, start your countdown timer and *make a mental note* of the speed setting on the treadmill. This will be the speed setting for your resting intervals.
- Start your countdown timer and increase the treadmill speed until

your cadence is up to 70+ and *make note* of the new speed setting on the treadmill and use the same setting for the next speed
interval. Keep your stride short and increase your arm swing as you
increase your cadence.

- After 1 minute, when your beeper goes off, reduce the treadmill
  speed to its original setting and do a 1-minute recovery walk.
- Alternate between the faster and slower settings on the treadmill
  for as many 1-minute intervals as your body feels comfortable
  doing. When you begin to sense difficulty with the increase in the
  treadmill speed, you're done for the day. Reduce the speed one last
  time to the slow setting and do a gradual cooldown for 10 minutes.

The Hill Workout

This workout is great if you're a flatlander and you're planning on
taking your dream trip to do some hiking in some faraway mountain
range. Or if you're going to spend a getaway weekend in San
Francisco. It's also a great workout to get you into your lower body and
out of your head. (If you do it at a faster speed, it can be a great cardio
workout.)

- Start slowly and warm up to a comfortable aerobic pace and a cadence of about 63 to 65 spm.
- Increase the incline of the treadmill. This is the equivalent of a
  hill workout and is a great way to get a good cardio workout without necessarily having to walk faster. Increasing the slope of the
  treadmill will increase the workload on your legs and subsequently
  elevate your heart rate. As you increase the slope of the treadmill,
  be sure to shorten your stride length and increase your cadence.
  Think of it as shifting to a lower gear to go up a hill, just like you
  would do in your car or on a bicycle.
- Increase the range of motion of your upper body (swing your arms
  in a bigger arc) while keeping your speed constant and your cadence quicker.
- Always keep your heels down. This keeps your calves from overworking.
- Raise the slope of the treadmill until it is difficult to keep your

heels down while striding, then back off just a notch until your
heels stay down with no effort.

- Walk with the treadmill at this slope until your legs begin to feel
some fatigue. Make note of the amount of time spent walking uphill so that you have a starting point for your next hill workout.

- Lower the treadmill back to level and continue walking at the
same speed for another 5 minutes and then cool down. One of these
workouts each week is plenty to keep your heart strong and your
hamstrings and calves well stretched.

OTHER INDOOR WORKOUTS

There are lots of other indoor alternatives if, like I said, you're willing
and creative. Getting a good walk into your schedule should never be
impossible. I've done everything from hill intervals in parking
garages to climbing stairs in hotels when I'm on the road. Here's a list
of places to go when you'd like to get in a walk but can't be outdoors.

SHOPPING MALLS

Here it is crucial for obvious reasons to have a focus to work on before
entering. This is an exercise in pinpointed focusing—and a great
Nonidentification exercise. Many years ago I worked in a downtown
office building and took my daily walks during lunch hour. My favorite walk was when I would think of a focus to work on and then try
to see how far I could walk before I lost the focus. Sometimes I would
keep it to the end of the hallway outside of my office. Many times I
would be able to hold it until I was a block away. I practiced this for
months and eventually got to the point where I could keep my focus
going continuously for 10 minutes. Never once was I able to complete
a walk without losing my focus, but it was an incredible challenge and
made me excruciatingly aware of how easily I could be pulled off my
center. It was and still is one of the best exercises I've ever found to develop a sense of centeredness while walking. I recently went for a
walk where I challenged myself to simply watch my in breaths and
out breaths without missing a single one. By the time I finally returned to my hotel room, I had watched every breath for 45 minutes

without a lapse and I felt as though I had done a very quiet, mindful moving meditation. I found myself in a state of centered calmness that was totally counter to the day I had just spent working a booth at a fitness expo.

This walk will give your body a good workout while *really* challenging your mind's ability to focus. I strongly suggest trying this exercise while walking through an indoor shopping mall. Pick a focus, a simple one that is easy to remember, like watching your breath. Then, before entering the mall, stand still for a moment and just watch your breath go in and out. Feel its rhythm, immerse yourself in it. When you feel solidly connected with your breath, set your countdown timer for 20 to 30 minutes and begin walking through the mall, watching each breath as if your life depended on it. Don't allow your focus to break for even one breath.

Your mind will have a typical field day looking at people and things, and wanting to attach itself to anything and everything. It loves distraction and would feed on it all day if you let it. So when your mind wanders, causing you to "miss" a breath, start over again by simply returning to watching each breath. Don't follow your thoughts and don't let your mind get in there and criticize you for losing the focus. Just go back to watching your breath and move on. Don't stop until your timer goes off. When it does, find a nice place to sit or stand and just *be* there in the quiet, feeling what you just accomplished.

STAIR CLIMBING

If you can call yourself a seasoned walker, this is a great cardiovascular workout and can be fun to do when you're traveling and stuck in a hotel with little time and nowhere to go for a workout.

Be sure to do your warm-up in a hallway. It's always better to start off on a flat surface before adding any amount of intensity to your walk. Walk for 5 minutes and then stand and do leg lifts, picking up your feet about 8 inches off the ground for another 5 minutes. Then move to the nearest stairwell and start up at what feels like a very relaxed pace—not too fast, you're still warming up. As you climb, keep your upper body directly over your leading foot *as you step onto the next stair.* This means that your upper body will always be tilted slightly forward over the edge of the upcoming stair. If you're too upright when climbing stairs you could risk overworking your hamstrings because you'll be pulling yourself up the stairs with each stride. Many times I'll even put my hands on top of my quads (just above the knees) and push down with each step. This allows my upper body to share in the work of climbing and keeps my legs from overworking. It is important to not hunch over as you try to stay over your leading foot, but instead keep your spine straight and your pelvis level. Walk up the stairs until you find it difficult to keep a steady pace. Then turn around and leisurely walk back down the stairs for a minute or until your heart rate drops back down into your aerobic zone. Then turn back around and head up again until you find it difficult to maintain a steady pace. Listen closely to your body. It will tell you when to go up and when to go down. When you're walking up the stairs, it is important to find a cadence that works for you, meaning that you can easily keep a steady, rhythmic rate going. For a great aerobic workout you can gradually increase your cadence on each ascent.

You can also practice using alternate groups of muscles while climbing stairs. If you go up the stairs in a slight zigzag, you'll bring in the use of the lateral abductors, which is great cross-training for hiking on trails.

AND DON'T FORGET . . .

Sports stadiums are another great way to get in a good workout and get out of the weather. The ramps leading up to the vendor concourses around the perimeter of ballparks are a great place to get a nice walk in inclement weather. Look for local gyms, YMCAs, or community recreation centers that have a basketball gymnasium. You can usually walk around the perimeter of the floor while being totally entertained by whatever is going on.

From here on out, whenever you are not inclined to walk outside, you'll have a few good ideas of what you *can* do. Walking indoors isn't only for the sake of exercise and fitness. It can be a way to move energy that is pent up in your body that *needs* to move. There is nothing better than a nice vigorous walk of any length that leaves you feeling you're back on an even keel. Play with these walks. Be open to the possibilities that they might create. And above all be willing to experiment with anything that you're drawn to doing when it comes to finding answers to your walking challenges in the great indoors.

CHAPTER TEN

Creating Balance in Your Diet

After a day's walk everything has twice its usual value.
—GEORGE MACAULAY TREVELYAN

S ound nutrition that supports body, mind, and spirit plays as important a role in your walking program as your training. In fact, there is no area of your life that will not benefit from healthy, nourishing foods. Eating a clean, high-octane diet allows you to gain access to greater amounts of chi, leaving you more energized, mentally focused, and enjoying an increased level of health. Good nutrition stabilizes mood swings, aids in weight loss, and will even help you to get a more restful night's sleep.

Unfortunately, for many people, food has become a loaded subject, fraught with peril. In an attempt to lose weight or become healthier, you may have already tried a variety of diets that confuse you about which foods are *good* for you and which foods will make you "fat."

Often it can feel like a bumpy ride up and down the hills of a low-carb, high-carb, low-fat, high-fat, high-protein roller coaster.

My passion for living a holistic lifestyle has led me into the study of foods and the practice of getting the most from the foods I eat. I've also been very fortunate to have found some great teachers along the way. What I've discovered is that just as I need to set up the right conditions in my ChiWalking program, I need to do the same in my dietary program to allow the chi to flow. My approach to diet has worked well for me for twenty-two years and I will share what I've learned to provide you with guidelines for creating your own healthy diet. Eating well is really based on the accumulation of chi. When your chi is flowing—whether from a stimulating walk or from eating fresh, wholesome food—you will be deeply nourished on many levels. Let's take a look at some of the basic principles that can help you set up the right conditions to get the most chi from your food.

FINDING BALANCE IN FOODS

Along with movement and stillness, *balance* is one of the three cornerstones of good health. When your nutrition is balanced, your energy is balanced and your chi is flowing. But let's face it—for one reason or another, most of us are out of balance. How do we get back into balance? Let's examine some of the common patterns that I see in my clients.

ALTERNATELY STARVING AND BINGEING

As I said above, food is an emotionally laden subject because of our cultural fixation on dieting to lose weight. This can lead to patterns of starving ourselves to lose weight and bingeing when we just can't take feeling hungry anymore. The solution is to eat enough nourishing foods to create a sense of balance in our bodies so that we never feel overwhelmed by hunger.

AN UNBALANCED BODY COMPOSITION

Many people are confused about the difference between having a thin body and a lean body. This is often the case for those who get stuck in the habit of alternately starving themselves to lose weight, then gaining it all back again whenever they return to their "normal" eating habits of fast-food meals, too many calories, too many sweets, et cetera. This pattern is known as yo-yo dieting.

The inherent imbalance in yo-yo dieting is the deterioration it causes in body composition, your percentage of body fat to lean muscle. When you severely restrict your caloric intake, your body is not getting the nutrients it needs to maintain and repair itself. Therefore, along with losing fat, you will also lose lean muscle because your body must literally cannibalize its own lean tissue to keep itself going. Over time, even if you become thinner, you might not really be leaner, because you will not be carrying a healthy amount of lean tissue on your frame, compromising your health and immune function. We have all seen those people who are thin but look as if they are made of flab and gristle. They may be thin, but they carry a high percentage of actual body fat per body volume.

The balanced way to lose weight is to not be in a rush. Take your time about it instead of starving yourself. Eat sensibly three times a day, increase your activity level, and make sure that you are always getting enough of all three food groups—especially protein—to maintain your lean muscle tissue. If you eat nutritiously, your body will naturally balance your weight over time.

Another cousin to starving and bingeing is *sporadic* eating—skipping different meals on different days, for example, eating three meals one day, then missing breakfast and lunch and eating a huge dinner the next day because you are about to drop dead from hunger. (Keep in mind also that eating a huge amount of food right before you go to bed because you are starved puts a strain on your digestive system and can cause restless sleep.) The balanced way is to spread your three meals evenly throughout the day and to eat enough of the *right type and amount* of food at each meal to satisfy hunger and stabilize metabolism. Your body loves consistency; that's the way it is designed by Nature. When the body doesn't know when its next meal is coming, it perceives that as trauma or famine and will adopt survival strategies such as slowing down your metabolism and hoarding fat as a protective mechanism. A slower metabolism can result in stagnant or lower levels of chi.

One aspect of balance that is high on the list of anyone trying to regulate their weight is between *calories eaten* and *calories burned*. If you want to lose weight, you have to eat fewer calories than you burn. If you want to gain weight, you have to eat more calories than you burn. It's a very simple formula that has been around since the time of the cavemen and a great example of applied thermodynamics. The one thing you must remember is to eat the right kinds of calories from clean, high-octane, nourishing foods.

ENERGY HIGHS AND ENERGY LOWS

When we don't fuel our bodies properly, skipping meals or eating fast foods or processed foods that have little nutritional value, we feel exhausted. Who among us hasn't experienced that late-afternoon slump that sends us running to Starbucks to grab a mocha and a Cranberry Bliss Bar? The balanced way is to eat nourishing foods three times a day to keep our blood sugar levels even, our energy consistent, and our flow of chi steady.

FEAR OF ONE OF THE THREE BASIC FOOD GROUPS

Today's low-fat, low-carb, or high-protein diet fads have made most of us afraid to eat certain nutrients that our bodies need for energy and tissue repair. The balanced way is to eat an appropriate amount of each of the three food groups and to make clean and nutritious fat, carbohydrate, and protein choices. I will explain more about this shortly when I discuss the food pyramid that forms the foundation of my approach to healthy eating and represents the best of what I have learned over the years.

OVERTAXING THE DIGESTIVE SYSTEM

When we are tired out, stressed, or haven't eaten in a long time we have a tendency to eat too much at one sitting, gobble our food, or reach for quick-fix foods that aren't really nutritious (such as throwing a pepperoni pizza in the microwave at 9:00 at night—a prescription for heartburn). These eating patterns result in our feeling bloated and experiencing digestive difficulties. The balanced way is to spread out your three meals throughout the day so that you are never collapsing with starvation before you sit down to eat. If you do not let your eating patterns be ruled by overwhelming hunger, you will be able to focus on preparing nourishing meals of satisfying and wise nutritional choices.

It is also important to remember that the digestive system is periodic. It needs time to rest from its labors between meals and during the night while *you* are resting.

COTTON AND STEEL

When we are starting out on a new food program, one of the most important things we must let go of is our identification of ourselves as being ruled by certain food choices that have not served us in the past. It is easy to get stuck on an idea about ourselves and our diet that is not based on a true understanding of what our bodies really need.

Anytime you are overidentified with a certain idea about what you must eat to be happy, you are using your ego and not your body to guide your decisions. Some examples include statements such as: "I'm addicted to chocolate—I can't live without it," "I just can't get going in the morning without my coffee," "If I don't eat meat every day, I won't have the strength I need," "If I don't eat bread at every meal, I will still feel hungry," and so on.

Learning the difference between what you think you want and what you really need involves a principle known as Cotton and Steel: gather to your center and let go of all else. Becoming mindful of your diet is the first step toward learning to let go of foods and eating habits that no longer serve you, your walking activities, or your health.

I love cheese. I could eat lots of it every day, but it wreaks havoc on my body. When I eat too much of it I get a stuffy head and feel like a slug. So I limit myself to having cheese four times a week because that's how much I can eat it without feeling like a phlegm factory. As the principle of Cotton and Steel states: gather to your center (my knowledge that too much cheese isn't good for me), and let go of all else (the other times during the week when I crave cheese). Anytime you gather to your center, you gather chi.

BODY SENSING VERSUS FOOD CRAVINGS

As the example above shows, an important step toward Nonidentification with any food we think we *have* to have is to take the time to observe our body's reactions to that food. This brings us to the subject of food cravings.

Why do we crave foods that aren't good for us, such as sugar and caffeine? The answer is that long-term poor nutritional patterns have thrown our bodies out of balance with regard to energy. When we reach for a candy bar or a cup of joe, we are actually trying to get back into balance, i.e., feel some energy coursing through us once more so that we can finish our afternoon at work or get dinner for the kids.

There are many things that can throw the body into a state of imbalance, such as too many sweets, too much protein, too many fried foods, or eating foods that have little or no nutritional value, such as fast foods and processed foods. Our society seems driven by sweets and desserts. Sugar can be found in everything, especially processed foods and low-fat foods. How do you think they get the flavor in low-fat foods? By adding hidden sugars. Otherwise, these foods would have no flavor. You may not recognize "sugar" in the long list of ingredients, but it is there under a new disguise. Eating so many quick-burning sugars can send your blood sugar through the roof and then let you down with the subtlety of an auctioneer's gavel. The all-American diet also seems to contain some form of meat at least once a day; that's way more animal protein than your body actually needs. And our culture is hooked on saturated fats, which come mainly in the form of fried foods; processed cooking oils; pastries containing butter, eggs, and oils; and animal products—especially meats such as beef and pork, which have a high fat content. A little bit of these foods is fine, but the amount that many people eat is out of balance with their body's real needs.

Because of poor eating habits that do not provide our bodies with proper nourishment, we often find ourselves craving the *opposite* of what we really need. For example, we might find it difficult to get rolling in the morning without coffee because our poor eating habits have caused low blood sugar problems and restless sleep. We crave a candy bar or chocolate brownie in the late afternoon because we didn't eat a nutritionally balanced breakfast and lunch. Our body has run out of fuel and needs a quick surge of energy, which it knows it can get from simple sugars.

Here we return to the concept of Cotton and Steel. To understand what you really need, you have to learn to differentiate between the false body, which is looking for a quick fix, and the informed body, which is nutritionally balanced and therefore sends you signals for what you really need to eat to maintain that balance. To get in touch with the informed body, I suggest that you try the food program offered in this chapter. Over the years I have seen this way of eating work with hundreds of clients, helping them to get their bodies back into balance and increase their flow of chi. At first, you may have to offer some resistance to cravings for foods that are not good for you, but as your body becomes more balanced, those cravings will become more manageable until they subside. As your blood sugar levels stabilize and you are eating enough nutrients daily to maintain and repair lean tissue, you will be able to hear the informed body loud and clear. Your body will ask for what it really needs, not a quick fix to rescue you from the low-blood-sugar ghetto.

THE PYRAMID

One of the tools I always give to my clients is the ChiWalking version of the Food Pyramid. This food program is designed to give you a very strong foundation in foods that deliver the most chi in proportion to the least amount of energy required to process them. As you move up through the levels of the pyramid, you will find foods that you still need in your diet, but in lesser amounts and with the awareness that more of these kinds of foods is not better. To support good digestion and a high level of chi, these foods need to be consumed in a smaller proportion to those at the base of the pyramid. The pyramid serves as a visual reminder of where our strength really comes from and shows the relative importance of certain types of foods in our lives.

This is certainly not the old official federal-government-issued Food Pyramid. Instead, it is based on what I've learned from my teachers and the diet I've been enjoying with great results for more than twenty years. Keep in mind that these are only general guidelines. If you are a vegetarian or an endurance athlete, you'll need to modify this pyramid for your needs. If you have an illness such as diabetes or cardiovascular disease, I strongly urge you to show this pyramid to your doctor and see what modifications he/she would suggest.

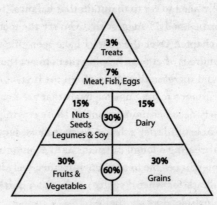

Figure 64—The ChiWalking Food Pyramid

LEVEL 1

In order for you to have a healthy, clean-burning fuel supply, the foundation of your diet (the base of your pyramid) should be made up of grains, fruits, and vegetables. Not only are fruits and vegetables a good source of clean-burning carbohydrate fuel, they also provide your body with much-needed antioxidants, which are free-radical scavengers. Free radicals in your cell tissues are produced by exercise and take much of the blame for everything from cancer to depletion of the immune system to premature aging. Whole grains are under-appreciated and underutilized in this culture. They are slow-burning carbohydrates that provide a steady, long-term source of energy. When whole grains are processed and refined they become fast-burning simple carbohydrates and low-octane fuel. My favorite whole grains are brown rice, kasha (buckwheat groats), oats, corn-meal, bulgur, and whole wheat bread. Fully 60 percent of my diet comes from Level 1 of the pyramid—30 percent from fruits and veg-etables and 30 percent from whole grains.

LEVEL 2

The next level of foods makes up 30 percent of my diet; 15 percent from nuts, seeds, and legumes (soy products, nut butters, dried beans, and lentils) and 15 percent from dairy (cheese, yogurt, and milk). If you're not into dairy or have problems digesting it, you'll need to make up for your lack of fat and protein with plant-based products. But if you are into dairy, keep it to only 15 percent of your diet. You need Level 2 foods in your diet in order to maintain strong chi in your system, but the quantity (30 percent) is half the amount of Level 1.

LEVEL 3

In my diet, the third level consists of meat, fish, and eggs, which I eat regularly but sparingly. It makes up a total of 7 percent of what I eat. I have fish once a week, meat once a week, and eggs one to two times a week. When animal protein is overconsumed, it depletes chi be-cause of the intense processing it requires. When you do eat meat, it should be the highest quality possible, and organic, when available. If you're a vegetarian, you'll get protein from plant-based sources such as legumes, and fats from oils, nuts, and nut butters.

LEVEL 4

Three percent of your diet should be from foods that are not necessar-ily eaten for nutritional reasons but are nourishing on other levels. I eat a yummy dessert once or twice a week, but when I'm tempted to eat too many sweets, I remind myself that I get more pleasure from having lots of chi than I do from being buzzed on sweets. There's no doubt about it, too much sugar depletes your immune system, creates energy highs and lows, and can quickly throw a solid pyramid out of balance.

Caffeine falls into this group. Although it has been proven to enhance mental alertness and improve performance, it is also a diuretic that increases water loss. If you mix caffeine with walking, take it with plenty of water.

FOODS TO AVOID

The following foods have little or no nutritional value and are not a part of the pyramid. This list includes such favorites as candy, condiments, processed foods, preservatives, additives, white flour (including bagels and most pastas), refined sugar, and sodas. Since these foods deplete your energy, it's best to get them out of your diet altogether.

PRACTICAL STEPS FOR A HEALTHY DIET

One of the most profound lessons I have learned over the years is the importance of food for a healthy lifestyle. Food affects every aspect of our being: how we age, how mentally alert we are, our mood, how much energy we have throughout the day, our activity levels, and our appearance—even the quality of our skin and hair.

If you are seeking to live a more holistic and balanced life, then it is important to consider how your diet fits into the larger scheme of things. To accomplish this successfully, it helps to be mindful not only of *what* you are eating, but also *how much* you eat, *when* you eat, and *how* you eat (the kind of environment in which you enjoy your meals).

WHAT TO EAT

If you want to have a high-quality life and walking program, then eat high-quality foods. Eating poor-quality foods is like putting low-octane gasoline into a fine sports car. The car will move, but it won't function at anywhere near its capacity. You will get a much higher performance out of your body if it's running on premium fuel.

Whenever you sit down to a meal, think about where the food you are eating came from and how it was processed or prepared and ask yourself the question, "How much life does this food have in it?" There can be no question that the most beautiful section of the grocery store is the produce section. It is always alive with vibrant colors and fresh smells because the foods there are filled with life. Compare this image with a supermarket aisle lined with cans and heavily processed foods wrapped in foil and plastic. Maybe the processed foods seem quick and convenient, but they have lost much of their nutritional value as they've been refined, bleached, freeze-dried, et cetera.

Fresh, wholesome foods don't need anything added to them to be perfectly aligned with your body's nutritional needs. Processed foods with their added flavors, colors, preservatives, and low-fat or low-sugar formulations aren't really an improvement on Nature. It's like taking a gorgeous landscape in Yellowstone Park and bringing in artificial flowers, fake trees, and stuffed birds. The setting is already perfect without those additions.

The best fruits and vegetables to eat are organic and fresh, grown without chemical fertilizers, pesticides, and fungicides. Ideally, it is a good idea to eat foods in season since they can be ripened and fresh picked locally versus being picked unripe and shipped to your market from thousands of miles away—using nonrenewable fossil fuels. For example, you can certainly buy strawberries from Chile or New Zealand in the winter months, but how much pleasure do you actually get from biting into a strawberry that is hard and lacks sweetness, deep color, and taste? It's also true that the closer to your home a food is grown, the more perfectly it matches your body chemistry.

Organic meats, eggs, and dairy are also your first choices because they are cleaner, come from animals that have been fed high-quality feed, and do not contain hormones, artificial colors, or other additives. If you love dairy but find that it gives you problems with phlegm, you may discover that you are able to eat organic cheese, milk, and other dairy foods with no difficulty.

Wild-caught fish are preferable to farmed fish, which are raised under conditions of extreme crowding, given antibiotics to keep them healthy, and often fed diets that contain more vegetable proteins because of the expense of feeding them fresh fish. This cuts down on their omega-3 and omega-6 content.

Once you begin eating organic foods you may find the taste so superior that you will never want to go back. For example, an organic chicken breast is not only flavorful but plump and juicy because the chicken it came from was not pumped up with water-retaining hormones before being taken to market. Organic poultry may cost more per pound, but you will have more chicken meat and less water residue left in your pan after cooking. An organic orange or apple will always be sweet, tart, and fragrant when you bite into it.

In summary, high-chi foods are:

- organic foods
- fresh foods
- freshly prepared foods
- locally grown foods

Low-chi or no-chi foods include:

- most canned foods
- overcooked foods
- processed and refined foods
- fried foods
- microwaved foods
- foods with additives, preservatives, or artificial coloring
- pickled foods
- condiments (commercially produced)
- smoked foods

HOW MUCH TO EAT

A great teacher set me up with my diet plan. I will always be grateful to him for allowing me to experience the power and chi of a well-designed food program. Here's an overview of how much food I eat.

I eat two main meals a day and one light midday meal. For breakfast, the most important meal of the day, I eat hearty. Three times a week I have a big bowl of hot whole-grain cereal loaded with nuts, seeds, and dried fruit (organic, since nonorganic dried fruits concentrate pesticides and often have preservatives and sugar added to them). My breakfast bowl holds about three cups of food, and I fill it to the brim. My wife Katherine's bowl holds about two cups. Once a week I have a substantial egg meal, and twice a week I have a grain and vegetable with nuts and sometimes cheese. Once a week I have a big bowl of yogurt with lots of nuts, seeds, raisins, and fruit.

At midday I eat a light lunch, which might include dried fruit with nuts, or fresh fruit with cheese, or peanut butter with vegetable slices.

My weekly dinner menu looks something like this: a meat meal once a week, fish once a week, a huge salad once a week, and beans and rice once a week. On the three other nights I have grain-and-vegetable meals, sometimes with nuts, seeds, and/or cheese.

I always get the freshest organic ingredients available. When you consider how much nutritional value you are getting out of fresh organic foods and how efficiently they repair and maintain the body, they are well worth the extra nickels and dimes they cost. These meals are simple, delicious, and wonderfully satisfying. And they will provide you with plenty of chi to support your walking program.

ACTIVITY, NUTRITION, AND WEIGHT LOSS

Many studies have shown that good nutrition coupled with movement will help you lose weight. Keep in mind, however, that increasing your activity level without nutritional support may make you thinner in the short run but will definitely not improve your body composition. Remember, you want to lose fat, not lean muscle, and to do that you must eat three nutritious meals a day containing appropriate amounts of lean protein, unsaturated fat, and complex carbohydrates.

Rather than seeing walking as a weight-loss activity—and evaluating your success only in pounds lost—I suggest that you use walking primarily as a focus for getting moving and becoming more healthy.

If you think of walking and nutrition as daily activities that give you pleasure and help create balance in your life, you will find it that much easier to make moving and eating a practice that can increase your general well-being, calm your mind, and expand your horizons.

WHEN TO EAT

Having high chi/energy is directly related to keeping your levels of blood sugar fairly even, without peaks and valleys throughout the day. For this reason, it is important that you don't skip meals and that you eat your meals at about the same time every day. This allows your stomach to work more efficiently because the cycles of eating, digesting, and resting are consistent. I eat my breakfast and dinner approximately twelve hours apart, with a light lunch in between, because that's roughly the amount of time it takes for my stomach to completely digest a meal. If I need an energy boost during the late morning or afternoon, I'll eat a piece of fruit with a tablespoon of organic or natural nut butter. Eating a fat with a simple sugar (fruit) keeps insulin from spiking and allows the body to completely utilize the energy instead of storing it as fat.

If you have health challenges such as type 2 diabetes or some other form of insulin sensitivity that makes it necessary for you to eat five or six smaller meals throughout the day, by all means do so. You can still avail yourself of the percentages of foods in the pyramid and the healthy, organic, high-chi foods that I suggest. Show the Food Pyramid to your doctor or nutritionist and allow him/her to help you modify it for your food program. And be especially careful to listen to your body.

GRADUAL PROGRESS

If you want to eat a cleaner, more wholesome diet, allow yourself and your body some time to develop new diet habits. Don't expect to have a perfect food program right away. Instead, be gentle with yourself and make small progressive changes, allowing yourself time to adjust. If you try to follow a food program that is too different from the one you are used to, it will be difficult to stick to and could cause some digestive stress. Instead, create good habits by making one change at a time and allowing these changes to become cumulative. Learning to eat nutritiously is like learning the ChiWalking focuses. They are easier if you practice them one at a time. Once each change becomes habit, you can add another brick to the foundation. Take your time and do it right. You will get the most chi from your food by being solid with each step along the way and moving forward with Gradual Progress.

For example, don't decide to stop eating sugar and drinking coffee the week you have to do your income taxes or prepare an important presentation at work. Just work on eliminating sugar, and when you're solid with that, begin to reduce your caffeine intake. The amount of chi gained by improving one aspect of your diet will give you the confidence to take on additional improvements.

Don't forget to listen to your body while you are modifying your food program. The Food Pyramid is only a suggestion, based upon my experience. You may find that you do better with a little more animal protein or that you just can't tolerate dairy at all. Allow your general health, sense of well-being, cravings (it's one thing to crave a candy bar, another thing altogether to crave a piece of fish or an egg), mood swings, energy levels, and sleep patterns to be your guide.

Again, if you are experiencing health challenges, show this chapter to your doctor or nutritionist and get his/her recommendations for how closely you should follow this program.

How to Eat

It stands to reason that the setting in which you eat your meals is as important as the quality of the food itself. If you are eating on the run, stuffing down your food, or trying to eat your meal in an environment of chaos, noise, and stress, you will create digestive difficulties and be unable to extract the chi you need from your foods. It is also likely that you will not get the right amount of food you need— or have the time to prepare the wisest selections under such stressful and hurried circumstances.

Sometimes we just can't help eating our meals under less than ideal conditions. If you are rushing toward a deadline at work or dealing with family emergencies, it might feel like an accomplishment just to eat a meal. But most of the time you *do* have a choice about the setting in which you eat your meals. Like your walking program, mealtime can become a time for mindful practice, a time when you settle yourself and consciously replenish your energy stores.

I have found that transitioning into a meal is the best way to get off to a nourishing start. First, make your eating environment a clear and settling space. Remove any semblance of chaos from your dinner table. Turn off the TV and the loud music. If you want sound, play soothing instrumental music and keep the volume low. Put down a beautiful place mat, use your favorite dishes and glassware, light a candle, or put a nice flower arrangement on the table. Make sure you have everything you need for your meal before you sit down so that you won't have to get up once you've started to eat.

Take a little time to remember what you're doing—you're taking in nourishment. Some people like to observe a moment of stillness to help them transition between their busy day and their time of nourishment. Others like to say a silent prayer of gratitude. I like to think about all the people whose hands helped the food to get to my table.

The way you begin your meal sets the pace for how it will unfold. As in your walking, start off slowly. If you start off too fast, gobbling your food, the whole meal will be fast. You'll finish with a full belly, but you won't feel nourished because your brain and body chemistry will not have time to catch up to your food intake. Your food will not be well chewed and sufficiently filled with enzymes from your saliva, so your stomach will have to work harder to digest it in its rough state. Instead of feeling vibrant and replenished when you get up from the table, you'll most likely feel like a toad. Eat slowly and take small bites. Sit up straight and remember to breathe between bites. (Do I sound like your mother yet?)

Eating in a pleasing and soothing setting with true respect for your body and the foods you eat is paramount to maintaining a high-quality lifestyle. Eating well *really* matters. It is the foundation for a successful walking program, a healthy body, and a vibrant life.

CHAPTER ELEVEN

The Choice Is Yours

Now shall I walk
or shall I ride?
"Ride," Pleasure said.
"Walk," Joy replied.
—W. H. DAVIES

n *ChiRunning*, I talked about Tiger Woods, who, just a few years into his unbelievably successful professional career, supposedly went into a "slump." He stopped winning. But what really happened was that Tiger realized his golf swing could be better and he decided to completely revamp it. After spending the next eighteen months working on his swing, Tiger came back stronger and better than ever, and was once again winning.

Well, two years later, as I'm sitting here writing this book, Tiger has just won the Masters again, after another supposed "slump" where he had a streak of ten major tournaments without a win. The true story was released to the media: Tiger did it *again*. He risked his career, risked his reputation, and realized he needed to "improve" his swing again. It took a couple of years, but now he's back winning and once again stronger and better than ever. While revamping his swing for the second time, he was under the pressure of the media and his fans to be winning, but he remained true to his own process. As stated in *USA Today*, "Woods refuses to budge from his stance of preaching patience." And, par for the course, he was right.

Tiger is one of my heroes. Not because he's a good golfer, but because he is a true student and master of his own body, constantly choosing to better his skills at every opportunity. That's how I want to be when I grow up.

My T'ai Chi teacher, Master George Xu, is the same way. About every two years he returns to China to visit with his grandmasters so that he can upgrade his own techniques. As he was preparing to leave for his most recent trip for more "schooling" he told me what it was like to be taught by some of the highest-level T'ai Chi masters in the world and what he was expecting to happen.

"They're going to put me in the toilet," he said in a very excited tone of voice. That was his endearing way of saying that they would make him aware, in no uncertain terms, of all the flaws in his technique. They would then explain to him the nature of each of those flaws until he had a clear understanding of what he would need to do to make the necessary changes. Throughout our conversation I never once perceived a sense of dread or fear in his voice. Instead, I detected a distinct sense of joyous anticipation. If I'd been in his shoes, I'd have been dealing with a serious case of performance anxiety. Not George.

When George returned from his trip to China, he was lit. He could hardly wait to practice and pass on all the inside secrets his teachers had passed on to him. In contrast to his usual grounded and methodical self, he had a palpable excitement bubbling out of him. I can only compare it to the level of excitement I'm met with when I tell Journey I'm taking her out for an ice cream cone (or when she wakes up on Christmas morning). It was like someone had just told him the biggest secret in the world and he could hardly wait to share it.

But what I appreciate most about Master Xu is that he is relentlessly pursuing a path of physical, mental, emotional, and spiritual mastery with his T'ai Chi practice. For him, there is nothing on the planet that he would rather be doing than practicing to improve the flow of chi through his body, and he has dedicated his life to teaching his students how to do the same. His own life and approach to learning are an extension of his T'ai Chi practice because there are no blocks to his forward movement.

George and Tiger have something in common. They both have an incredibly healthy attitude toward learning because they are both clearly aware of *what they don't know* and are both willing to choose to grow beyond that state, no matter what it takes. They're not just seeking information, they're seeking to be masters of their minds and bodies. Their approach to learning is based on their excitement around learning more body knowledge. I admire their ability to be at the "top of their game" and still have the wherewithal to return to school if that is what is called for. They both have an innate ability to consistently choose for the higher.

I can see a similar enthusiasm in my students and in the thousands of people I see out there at walking events who are often raising money for great causes. They're out there having a great time and improving their health and being an inspiration to their friends and family.

THERE'S MAGIC IN YOUR SHOES

Walking is currently enjoying a resurgence in popularity, and for good reason. The word is out: walking is the simplest, most convenient way to get our sedentary society moving, active, and healthy once again. Just like Dorothy in *The Wizard of Oz*, we're realizing that there's magic in our shoes and they can take us to places we never dreamed possible. But instead of merely clicking our heels, we're putting one foot in front of the other and taking back our health.

Walking has been scientifically proven to be effective at

- dramatically reducing the risk of death;
- lowering the risk of heart disease;
- lowering blood pressure;

- losing weight;
- increasing mental acuity;
- improving balance;
- reducing the risk of dementia;
- reducing the risk of breast and other types of cancers;
- relieving the symptoms of major depression;
- warding off diabetes;
- increasing bone density;
- increasing your sex drive;

. . . the list goes on! And you can enjoy all of these benefits, and so many more intangible ones, with a 3- to 5-hour-a-week walking program. I've said it before and I'm going to say it again, walking is a magic elixir for your health. It is an accessible, inexpensive, no-frills, drugless way to address the spiraling number of health problems that plague our nation today.

This morning I took a hike up Mount Tamalpais, of whose presence the residents of Marin County are constantly aware. Its beauty is loved and enjoyed by children and adults alike. Its peak protects us from the storms coming off the Pacific Ocean. Its broad base provides us with a constant reminder of being grounded and solid in ourselves, while its misty peak urges us to reach for the sky and the unknown. When I reached the peak, I realized that from this 360-degree vantage point, of which I was in the center, I had a *lot* of options, not only for what I could do with my day, but also for what I could do with my life. I looked out at the ocean and imagined traveling. I looked at the city and thought about all the creative activity going on in San Francisco. I looked down at my little neighborhood, tucked away behind a hill, and felt a sense of belonging somewhere. I chose to come home and work on this chapter with Katherine, and I deeply knew that it was the best choice. I also knew that those other options would still be there.

If there is any one step of the Five Mindful Steps that I think is most important, it is Making a Choice. Actually, it's not "most important," but it is the culmination of getting aligned, engaging your core, and creating balance. The first three steps prepare you to make a choice from the very best possible vantage point. Then, making a choice seems effortless and everything is in place for you to move forward easily and gracefully. Even gravity becomes your ally. When you make a choice from a deep, centered place within, and with the foundational support of having taken the right steps, nothing can stop you.

Index